Copyright © 2019 Cheesecake LLC

info@stephaniemillsbooks.com

I Don't Share Cheesecake – First Edition, v1 – July 2019

I Don't Share Cheesecake

...because my life is too good to share with just anybody

Stephanie Mills

ACKNOWLEDGEMENTS

To my best poodle, Kate, who I'm sure, would sue me if I didn't make sure the world knew that she came up with the title of this book. Over a burger and a beer with a couple of friends, Kate just blurts out, "I don't know why you can't just call it, *I Don't Share Cheesecake*". Kate contributed so much to this book. She stuck with me through the dark times and encouraged me when I wanted to give up. Kate, we have been through some rough stuff and some hilarious stuff. Through our 26 year friendship, we have managed to get through everything life threw at us with laughter and came out stronger together. Love you Kate.

Special thanks to my mom and dad who are completely responsible for my inappropriate sense of humor.

My sisters Melinda & Joanna and my brothers-in-law, Matt and JP: Thank you for always exercising the above mentioned inappropriate sense of humor at the times when I needed it most.

To my first readers: Cynthia, Melinda, Noelle, Kate, Dennis and Dave. Thank you for taking time out of your lives to read a book from a rookie writer. Each one of you provided unique feedback that helped to shape my final edit. Some of your critiques were hard and there were some real battles in *do I* or *do I not* include this content. But it was those critiques that forced me to dig deeper and ultimately keep God involved in what I did and did not write about.

Holly, I am a better writer because of you. I will always be thankful for the time you spent helping me get started.

To my friend Bethany for the beautiful book cover! You stepped up at a time when my plan for this book completely fell apart, I had lost all direction and wasn't sure how I was going to finish. Thank you for your suggestions on how to make this book awesome and for your unwavering friendship.

Melissa   Schaefer   Photography www.melissaschaeferphotography.com

To my cat Simone, my little shadow, who curled up next to me (or on me) wherever and whenever I was writing.

NO thanks to my cat Sipowicz who meowed relentlessly every time I sat down to write.

To the casts of NYPD BLUE and How I Met Your Mother for the countless re-runs I had on in the background while I was writing and re-writing this book. And just in case this book finds the hands of Dennis Franz…sir, you are one of my favorite people!

Dave, where do I begin? I never thought we would meet over ducks and that you would be the one to take me to the finish line with this book. I have learned so much from you in the short time we have worked together. The enthusiasm you have for everything you do is so incredibly contagious. You are FUN to work with! Thank you for taking time out of your life to help me finish this project. I hope this is the beginning of many more projects together in the future. Check him out at www.developawesomeskills.com

And finally to my Heavenly Father, Jesus and the Holy Spirit (I never know which to address this to so I'll just cover all three) for the lessons learned in the loyalty of old friendships, the excitement of new friendships and the pain of friendships lost.

Scott Callender

Scott Callender is not in this book

Dedication

To my brother from another mother, my best friend, Dana.

Nobody made me laugh harder.

I miss your laugh.

Table of Contents

CHAPTER ONE

I hate being at a table alone, with a married couple. Talking about their married friends, and their married furniture. They're always trying to make me feel like their life is so much better than mine. You know, I have a very exciting life. It's very exciting.

~ Elaine, the TV show Seinfeld

What is it about being single that makes women feel so incomplete? God didn't make us half a person. Unfortunately, people and often the church itself can do a great job of making you feel incomplete if you're single. I have had pastors with the best of intentions say to me, "I just can't understand why you're not married yet." Or friends with the best of intentions tell me I'm too picky. Just the other day, a friend said to me, "Steph, we can't afford to be picky at our age." What a weird thing to say to me in front of your boyfriend...that actually happened.

Why do so many people act like marriage is the ultimate goal? I might not be married, but I have a lot of friends and family who are, and the more I watch them, the more serious the idea of marriage becomes in terms of commitment; especially basking in the freedom and advantages being single brings.

You are making a covenant to attach your life to somebody else through the good, the bad, and the really bad. There are days where his needs will take precedence over this week's episode of Criminal Minds. There is less freedom to have a spontaneous dinner with your girlfriends. You are no longer just "you." You're "us."

Once I began thinking about what marriage really meant, my perspective began to change. Being married is nothing to take lightly. Is there a man out there who would make me want to give up my single life? And am I the best version of myself for this man to give up his single life? And if so, what are our deal breakers? What are our expectations? I need to know. I've seen too many people go into relationships without having asked any hard questions. Some are too afraid to ask simple questions.

Too afraid to ask: You know what I'm going to miss after we're married? My skincare line. I've been using it for years, but it's really expensive.

Common sense: Why can't you have your skin care line after you're married?

Too afraid to ask: I think he might say it's a waste of money and I don't want to be *that* girl.

Common sense: You *think* he *might* say? You're getting ready to marry this guy. If you can't talk to him about that, what else are you not talking to him about?

The decision to wait on God was easy, but exactly *what* to wait on God for was not. I had to figure out what my part was and make sure I wasn't stepping on God's toes where His part is concerned. And what do I do while I wait?

I spent most of my life perfecting the phrase, "I'll do that after I'm married." I'll buy new furniture after I'm married. I'll travel more after I'm married. I even said I'll get a tattoo after I'm married. (I wouldn't want to ruin my wedding photos)

Has anybody else thrown this statement around? The problem is that my early 20's turned into my mid 30's and now here I am, approaching 40 and I'm still single with no light at the end of that tunnel.

No matter how confident you are in your singleness, there will always be somebody who looks at you with pity. Or worse, wonders what is so wrong with you that you're still single. This is where you have to

KNOW WHO YOU ARE because it is so very easy for those feelings to make room in your mind and before you know it, they've taken root in your heart.

So now when somebody asks me why I'm not married yet or says something stupid like "Don't worry, he's out there" (as if I asked...so annoying) my response to those people is now this: I haven't met anybody worth marrying yet. I take marriage and the covenant of attaching my life to another person very seriously, and I'm not going to settle for just anybody simply because I'm getting older.

It's not that I'm waiting for some unrealistically good looking man to show up on a motorcycle, say something romantic and fall stupid in love with me. There is no fantasy I'm holding out for. I just know what I want.

More importantly, I know what I don't want. I don't want to be called last minute for a date. I'm not somebody you call when you have nothing better to do. I believe if a man really wants to get to know me, he will be intentional in setting a date and following through. If he is lazy in pursuing me, I will assume he is not that serious, and I will move on.

And for the love of my sanity, he has to be direct with me. If you want to date me, tell me. If you don't want to put a label on it, then I am not the woman for you. I want the label. I won't be loosely committed to anybody. I'm an all-in woman.

My friend Pastor Jim always says, "A man of God knows how to pursue a woman and make his intentions clear. And a real woman of God will not make him compete." Did you hear that ladies? I'm calling you out too. I love men. The check-your-character moments in this book are for men and women.

And the Lord God said, "It is not good for man to be alone."

~ Genesis 2:18a

I heard a preacher once say that single people LOVE this verse and we do! It gives us hope when thoughts of unworthiness start to fill our minds for no reason other than feeling like there is no end to our singleness in sight.

Over the course of 6 years, God has slowly helped me change my attitude toward being single, and just when I think I'm good and content, He always shows me something new that manages to take me to a higher level of contentment.

I have said goodbye to feelings of loneliness and inadequacy and fully embraced this season of my life. I've learned that the combination of being transparent with others and being painfully self-aware has given me amazing perspective and has strengthened my faith and friendships in ways I never knew existed.

I no longer say I'll do that when I'm married. I'm waiting on God for the right man. I'm not waiting on God to enjoy my life.

Let's discuss a day that is hard for some single women, Valentine's Day. This will be good, stay with me.

I have never cared about Valentine's Day. I don't like crowded restaurants. I don't like giant, oversized stuffed animals. I know it sounds cliché, but it's true: I would rather be surprised with grocery store flowers on any other day of the year.

That doesn't mean we didn't celebrate it. But it was always very low-key. For one Valentine's Day, my last boyfriend brought me one red rose he got at CVS with a package of Oreo's. In all honesty, he could have just

13

brought me the Oreo's, and I would have been happy. You had me at Oreo's!

He figured out how little I cared when we had our first Valentine's Day together. He told me that day was entirely up to me. Wherever I wanted to eat and whatever I wanted to do. I thought about it for 10 seconds and said, "Chipotle and Blockbuster."

"Are you serious?"

"Yes."

"I just told you we could do whatever you wanted and that's what you picked?"

"Well, that's all I want to do."

With that said, during my single years, I would try to make sure that my single friends who *did* care about Valentine's Day had a special day. One year, I surprised my friend at work with homemade strawberry cupcakes and a giant card with an invitation to come over to my place for Chinese take-out and a movie.

Are we all on the same page? I don't care about Valentine's Day...until 2018 and I'm the last single one among my group of friends. I recognized this as a day that had the potential to bum me out. I had two options. I could cross my fingers and hope that somebody took the time to think about making this day special for me or I could make it special for myself.

I opted to make it special for myself.

So, what do I love? I like to read, I love Chinese food, and I love cheesecake. I left work early that day and drove to a mall about 30 minutes from my work. I planned this afternoon right down to what music I would listen to in the car. I danced to the album *Crazy Sexy Cool* by TLC on my drive in; a CD I haven't listened to in years. Yes, I still listen to my CD's.

This particular mall has the two things I wanted right next door to each other: Barnes & Noble and Cheesecake Factory. I went straight to Barnes & Noble, where I spent over an hour trying to decide which books I was going to buy. I could spend hours just browsing around in a bookstore, which is easy to do when you're single. There is nobody there telling you to hurry up. I left with three new books that day.

Then I walked next door to Cheesecake Factory and picked out not one but two slices of cheesecake because who can pick just one of their several amazing flavors? From there, I drove to my favorite Chinese restaurant that I always went to when I lived on that side of town and got an ungodly amount of food to go. On my drive home, I put in the CD *Something to Remember* by Madonna; another CD I haven't listened to in many years.

When I got home, I curled up on my couch with my Chinese food and cheesecake and watched two of my favorite movies: *A League of Their Own* and *Can't Hardly Wait*.

I had a great night! And I didn't wait for somebody else to make it great. I had a better night than some of my friends who are actually *in* a relationship which only proves that being intentional is just as important when you're single as it is when you're in a relationship. I was *intentional* in making this day fun for myself...and it worked! I did it again in 2019, and as long as I'm single, this is what my Valentine's Day will look like. I do look forward to the day when I can walk into Barnes & Noble with somebody holding my hand, but until then, I'll have fun doing it alone.

The point is you are allowed to have a good time when you're single. Sure it can be more fun sharing a good time with somebody, but it can also be fun when it's just you. Sometimes it's more fun that way. Nobody rushed me while I was browsing around in the bookstore. Nobody interrupted my movie night with boring stories about their day, and nobody asked me to share my cheesecake with them...I don't share cheesecake.

CHAPTER TWO

I never had any friends later on like the ones I had when I was twelve.

~ from the movie, Stand by Me

So what started all of this? It wasn't one defining moment that made me decide to stop waiting to get married to enjoy my life. It was a series of events that over time, got me to a place where I realized I had to make some changes.

My life started to take a turn in 2009. I was in a 3-year relationship with a man I thought was "the one." I was head over heels, stupid in love with him. When your life goal is to be in a relationship, you usually ignore any red flags that come up, and there were plenty of red flags; ones that he threw up and ones that I threw up. This isn't just about what *he* didn't do right; I wasn't right either. I was in love with the potential I saw in him, not with who he was at the time.

We had a lot of fun together and had a lot in common, like a shared love of music. He is also, by far, the best workout partner I ever had. Nobody pushed me harder at the gym than he did. As much fun as we had together, we didn't see eye to eye on a lot of the important things like faith, morals, going to church and simple things like give-and-take in a relationship.

There were many times where I realized this was not the best God had for me (which also means I wasn't God's best for him), but I ignored it because at that time in my life it was better to be in the *wrong* relationship than to be in *no* relationship. I figured as long as I kept my head down and acted like the world's most amazing girlfriend, he would never have cause to leave me.

From April to July 2009, I was a juror on a sentencing trial for the brutal murder of a two-year-old girl at the hands of her father. This trial was an incredibly emotional time for me. I spent weeks in court looking at a man who murdered his two-year-old baby girl. The crime scene photos are still etched in my brain to this day. I was sworn not to talk about the trial to anybody outside of the juror room. We couldn't talk to other jurors about it at our lunch break and were not allowed to show emotion on our faces in the courtroom. I spent a lot of my time writing my feelings down in the notebook I had with me when court was in session.

This trial drew me closer to God because God was the only one I could talk to during that time. I was driving home from court one day toward the end of the trial, and I had a thought. It was a nagging thought. Something I felt I was supposed to pray. The very idea of this prayer terrified me. I've been a Christian my whole life, but at this time in my life, I was very much living for myself.

The question was, did I want what *I* wanted, or did I want what *God* wanted?

I recall a lot of fear at that moment thinking about the prayer that kept coming to my mind, yet out of my mouth, I prayed, "God, I really love this guy. But if he isn't the one you want me to be with, you're going to have to remove him from my life because I'm not going to leave him."

One week after the trial ended, He did. He sat down on the sofa next to me one night while I was watching TV. I laid my head on his shoulder, and he said, "I think we should break up." It was completely out of nowhere! There was no big fight leading up to it; it was over.

The four-month jury trial had just ended leaving me emotionally drained, and now my three-year relationship was over. Two weeks following that breakup, my only cat died. (Perfect)

I spent the next four months feeling very sorry for myself. I became bitter and angry. I couldn't look at any relationship without thinking, it might look good now, but I wonder when that will end?

That Christmas, I went to my home state of Minnesota. One night, I went to a local Buffalo Wild Wings with my friends Amanda and her husband Chuck and Scott and his then-girlfriend (now wife) Becky for dinner.

I met Amanda at school in 1989. I swear every time we get together, there is a window where we turn into those kids who have a 13-year-old boy sense of humor. It's usually the two of us on the sofa in her house laughing our asses off at God knows what while one of her kids asks "What's so funny?" and Amanda fires back "We are!"

We only went to school together for three years but always stayed close. Even after I moved to Arizona in 2002, she is somebody I see every time I go back home without fail. Her girls (they're adults now which freaks me out to say) are more like nieces to me. People always say that friendships formed in high school rarely make it into adulthood. I guess I'm lucky. This year Amanda and I are celebrating 30 years of friendship, and it was not always easy. We walked through some hard stuff together, but we never let go of each other. That's why we're still friends today.

Scott and I had a different beginning. I met him in 1996 when we worked together at McDonald's. We were night and day different from each other. I went to church, attended a private school, and was pretty self-righteous in my late teens. Scott was obnoxious; he partied a lot and appeared always to be one bad decision away from getting into legal trouble.

We were at a party one night in our late teens. There was a group of us in the kitchen playing cards and another group in the living room. On this particular night,

Scott had a lot to drink. Some of us call it, *The Hot 100 Incident.* I was sitting on the kitchen counter, stone sober (because my dad was a cop and I didn't dare drink before I was twenty-one years old) when Scott stumbled into the kitchen. He badgered me often for going to parties and never drinking.

Scott: JEFF! JEFF!

Me: Are you talking to me?

Scott: Yes.

Me: My name is Steph.

Scott: Jeff, Steph, whatever. You gotta try this stuff.

Just last year, Scott and Becky were in Arizona, and we had made plans to go to a dueling piano bar. As we left their hotel room for the evening, I headed down the hall with my friend Kate and Becky behind me. Once I heard their hotel room door close, I heard fast footsteps coming up behind me. It was Scott.

When he caught up with me in that hotel hallway, he put his arm around me and said, "I love you, Jeff." Yes, after twenty-some years, he still calls me Jeff.

I was going through a dark time in my life the night I met up with these friends for dinner. I was a mess! I was also surrounded by friends who I've known for many years, and they were not going to let me sit in this negative space for very long. I was talking (more like complaining) about the last few months. I must have been a real mess because I remember like it was yesterday the words my friend Becky spoke to me.

"This isn't you. You have to find a way to get back to the person you used to be."

She was right. This wasn't me. I was a happy, funny, the-glass-is-always-half-full kind of person. I was always laughing. I love laughing. I hadn't laughed in months. Instead of enabling my self-pity, Becky called me out on it.

Take a minute and evaluate your friendships. In 2009, Becky wasn't even a friend I had known for very long. I had only known her for about a year and a half, and she was already dropping hard truth bombs on me (in love). That's gutsy. That's also the kind of people I try to surround myself with. You have to be able to take hard truth from people who love you, or you'll never grow.

If you don't have friends like Becky in your life, it's time to find some. Make sure you're not surrounded by a bunch of takers; people who are always looking to get something from you but never give anything of substance to your life.

I have some takers in my life too but hear me out. I believe they're usually placed in your life for a reason. Be there for them. Show them the love and grace that they may not have ever experienced before in their lives. Help them become better people. However, at some point, these takers should become givers. Some of my most amazing friendships started as takers.

There are also some people who are there to take advantage of you. You have to use wisdom when it comes to people like that. I'm not saying you should only be friends with people who do something for you. Giving back is a great thing! There should always be somebody in your life that you're giving to in one way or another whether it be your money, your time, your amazing personality, or like Becky is for me, support, encouragement and a good kick in the ass. Just be aware of those who only take advantage of you.

21

Friends who walk with you during a storm are worth keeping around. By calling me out, Becky was walking with me. It was time to change.

January 2010, I started attending church again regularly. I mean every Sunday morning as well as an additional class after service, where I made some amazing friendships. I poured myself back into the faith I was not only raised with, but I believe in my heart to be true. I found new friends, my heart began to heal, and I started to laugh again.

November 15th, 2010

It was a typical day at work when my cell phone lit up. It was my friend Kate. Why was she calling my cell phone during work hours? That's not like her at all.

"Hello?"

"Stephanie, I have some really bad news."

I quickly stood up from my desk and started saying, "NO-NO-NO-NO-NO-NO!" I could hear it in the tone of her voice that what she was about to say was going to dramatically change my life forever.

"It's Dana. He was in a really bad car accident."

I'm thinking, okay, so what? Did he break his leg? He needs emergency surgery...

She continued, "He didn't make it. He died."

I left my desk, Kate still on the phone, and headed toward the door. My brain was trying to process what I had just heard, but my body wanted to collapse. As I made my way toward the door, the room started spinning, and I fell into a filing cabinet, catching myself with my one free hand. I couldn't stop shaking. All I could get out was, "Dana? Are you sure? Dana?"

Once I got off the phone with Kate, I found myself in the bathroom at work, sobbing. I sat there shaking and crying out, "God, I don't get it. I just don't get it. What are we going to do without him?"

Dana. He wasn't just some guy I knew. He was my best friend; my oldest friend. While my earliest memory of him was about age 5, we actually go back as far as the church nursery. We were born twelve days apart. We went to the same school, Kindergarten through 12th grade. The shenanigans and endless laughter that ensued every time Dana was present is something that my heart misses more than anything else in the world. Shenanigans still ensue when I'm around (ask any of my friends), but I often wonder how much more fun would it be if Dana was alive.

He had this piece of crap car in high school that was so old the floor of the car had parts that were rusted right through. Any time Dana drove somewhere, he would hold out his hand toward his crappy car and make the noise "beep-beep" as if he were disarming a car alarm. It always made me laugh!

For a time, he and another friend of ours worked overnights at a local grocery store in Elk River, Minnesota that is no longer there, called Ron's Foods. I worked half a mile down the road at McDonald's. On the nights when I closed, I would drive to Ron's Foods, and the three of us would sit around and talk into the early morning hours. Whenever I'm in Minnesota, I think about that every time I drive by what used to be that grocery store.

We would go bowling for hours on Friday nights! After I graduated high school, I joined a couple of bowling leagues with a guy I was dating at the time. Because of that, the owner, George (who also taught me to bowl) gave me a nice discount when I would come in on non-league days. Dana and I would meet up, sometimes with other friends, and bowl for hours while George yelled at me from the front counter, "Keep your wrist straight!"

Dana eventually signed up for YWAM which is an evangelical, interdenominational, non-profit Christian missionary organization. He asked me to do it with him to which I quickly responded with, "no thanks." I was perfectly happy with my life at the time and didn't feel much like branching out. I had a boyfriend and just started a new career in Insurance. Traveling abroad wasn't my thing at that time in my life.

I remember one weekend he came home from YWAM for a visit. I was in the basement of my parents' house when I heard his voice as he ran down the stairs, "What up, Mills!" I screamed, "You're back!" quickly turned around, started down the hall toward him, and then I stopped...

Me: What did you do to your hair?

Dana: You don't like it?

Me: No.

Dana: Well, so what. Jessica likes it.

Dana met his wife Jessica at YWAM. The summer they got engaged, Dana asked me, and another friend ours, to drive to Kansas City (where he was currently living) so we could meet her. We loved each other, fought with each other, and talked to each other like a brother and sister would. I'll never forget the phone call a day or two before we were supposed to leave for Kansas City.

Dana: Do you think you can come here and not-be-you for a weekend?

Me: What the hell does that mean?

24

Dana: That, right there, where you just run off at the mouth!

Me: Why do you even want me to come if you're so worried she won't like me?

Dana: 'Common Mills (he called me Mills), I really like this girl.

This was completely new territory for me; Dana and his fiancé. My best-guy-friend was getting married. How does this work? Can I still call him? Can we still be friends? It took some time and a few missteps to figure things out, but I think we were all very gracious with each other when we messed up and had to create new boundaries. I think we all learned from that experience, and it's no longer a mystery to me how to navigate a guy/girl friendship when one gets married or starts dating.

As it turns out, Jessica and I had something in common; the TV show, The Golden Girls. We spent our first night together on a pull out sofa bed watching re-runs of that show. If memory serves me, I believe Jessica is the one who called to tell me they got engaged. I vaguely remember a phone call from Dana, "I proposed to Jessica." I said, "I know, Jessica told me." He gave an annoying sigh and said, "I gotta go."

Sorry guys, but when a male friend of mine goes and gets paired off with an awesome woman, the odds of the friendship shifting a little is inevitable. Closing in on nine years after Dana's death, I still consider Jessica, a very dear friend of mine.

The last time I saw Dana was Sunday, August 15th, 2010. I was in town for my grandma's funeral. Jessica and I had made plans to meet up for coffee that morning. She said Dana had been working long hours and she wasn't sure if he would make it or not but either way, she wanted to see me. It had been three years since I saw either of them.

7 am that morning, my last morning before flying back to Arizona, Dana called.

"Can you meet me in half an hour?"

"Yes!"

I quickly threw myself together and drove Caribou Coffee in Elk River. I got there first and had just sat down when, for some reason, I decided to take a picture of my coffee with my cell phone. Just then I heard Dana say,

"Did you just take a picture of your coffee?"

"No."

"Oh, so you're a nerd and a liar."

"Alright, shut up."

I looked around and saw Dana was alone. I asked where Jessica was, and he said she was going to meet up with us later. It was just Dana and me alone for three hours. I hadn't spent time alone with him since before he met Jessica. For three hours, we talked about what was new in our lives, the dreams we had and what our next plans for life were. It felt like the first adult conversation we had ever had.

I made a big deal about the fact that I got three hours alone with him that day. I couldn't explain it then, but I recognized it as something very special. Jessica and the boys showed up for the last fifteen minutes or so that we were there. I sat in my chair smiling as I watched those young boys climb all over their dad, and suddenly it was as though there was nobody in the room but him and his boys. His attention went right to them completely.

Just then, I heard the Holy Spirit say to me, "You need to make a better effort with those boys." I knew that was true, but it didn't have as significant an impact on me at the moment as it would three months later.

We walked out to our cars together, hugged, exchanged a "love you," and he said, "Call us when you know what dates you'll be home for Thanksgiving. Maybe we can get everybody together for a BBQ or something" "Yes, sounds like a plan."

And that was the last time I saw Dana alive.

The way Jessica carried herself during those couple of years after Dana's death was nothing short of extraordinary. The second I got home from Dana's funeral, I began praying for a husband for her. We walked through a very tough time together, and nobody was happier for her than I was when she met somebody new.

When I got the call, I wasted no time buying a flight to Minnesota to attend her wedding. I have a lot of respect for her. I treasure her friendship and am thankful every single day that she is still in my life.

To this date, Dana's death is the most traumatic event ever to take place in my life. It hurt like hell when he died. I have two younger sisters. Dana was the brother I never had. My brother died.

My sister Joanna came to visit me over my 40th birthday, and we put up a ton of decorations in my apartment. I left those decorations up after my birthday ended and through what should have been Dana's 40th birthday. My best friend Kate came over that day, and we ate cupcakes and watched one of his favorite movies, Dumb & Dumber.

Dana's mom, Jeanine, said something that has stuck with me over the years:

"People keep saying it'll get better, and they mean well, but if I cut my arm off it isn't going to get better. But I will learn to live without it."

And she's right. It didn't get better; just different. You don't get over losing somebody like that, but you do learn to live without them. Over time, the pain was no longer as surface as it once was. Now I have a good cry once or twice a year, but I still think about him every single day.

Spring 2011

Of course, it is happening inside your head, Harry, but why on earth should that mean that it is not real?

~ Harry Potter and the Deathly Hallows

At this point, I had been actively involved in my church for a year and a half. I was a regular greeter and usher for just about every service we had. I met a lot of new people and made some great friends during that time. Something else was beginning to rise up in me as well; Anxiety.

Unless you've personally experienced anxiety attacks, there isn't much you can do to help someone who is battling it. Telling someone to get a grip on their

28

emotions or to stop stressing out doesn't work. Some people think anxiety is brought on by stress and worry. The truth, for me, was the exact opposite. It wasn't until the attacks started that the worry and stress began.

Anxiety is a funny thing. The symptoms were minor at first. Ringing in my ears, clammy hands, cold sweats, and they usually passed after a few seconds. Then one day, they all came at once and on a grander scale. Blurry vision, dizziness, and nausea, and it was almost always while I was at work and completely out of nowhere. I would calmly leave my desk and go for a walk outside and pray. It helped a little but never completely left my body.

I had been through a hurricane of "life stuff" in the last two years. The jury trial, both my cats died, a relationship with a man I thought was "the one" suddenly came to an end which sent me on a path of recommitting my life to God and doing things His way and then for reasons which I will never understand, my oldest friend dies suddenly in a car accident. No wonder anxiety set in.

But not everybody sees it that way. For some reason, when it comes to anxiety or other types of mental illness, there is always a group of Christians who want to make it your fault. "If you would just read your Bible more" "If you really trusted God you wouldn't be battling this" and then there's my personal favorite, "What sin in your life is bringing this on?"

It's so completely absurd to say something like that to a person who is battling something that to them, is very scary. Not to mention the fact that it's just not biblical. God, never one time promises to keep us from personal storms in our life, but He does promise to walk us through them.

Here on earth, you will have many trials and sorrows. But take heart, because I have overcome the world.

~ John 16:33b

After a few months of trying to handle this in my own strength, I got on the phone with a friend who told me she didn't think I had fully grieved Dana's death. What does that even mean? Is it possible to fully grieve a loss of that magnitude and how do you know when you've "arrived"?

At this point, it had been six months or so since Dana's death. Every time I felt sadness or tears come on, I pushed them back down. I didn't notice it at the time, but I believe the irrational thoughts that went through my mind were halting the grieving process.

(Internal Dialogue) "What gives you the right to be this sad after six months? You're not his wife, or brother, or parent. Get over it already."

Pushing down my feelings wasn't working. I had two choices: I could have a moment with God and get to the root of these anxiety attacks, or I could go to the doctor and get a pill to eliminate the symptoms.

Now I have nothing against meds. I have good friends that take them, and it has helped them tremendously, but for me, I wanted to exhaust every possible avenue before I even considered seeing a doctor...and I was SO close to seeing a doctor. It was bad.

I got home from work and had a typical evening. Cleaning, dinner, TV...I knew what I needed to do, but I didn't want to face the pain that came with that. Finally, after the sun had set, I shut the TV off and sat curled up on my sofa in the dark. I immediately started crying. I cried so hard. I didn't know where this process would lead me; I just trusted I would find my way. And I did.

I went back to 2007 when a mutual friend of mine and Dana's disappeared from our lives. It wasn't anything that we did; he was just going through some stuff at the time and withdrew. I had reached a point where I was done contacting this person. Dana was still reaching out on occasion, and he was frustrated with the fact that I had stopped.

As we left that Caribou Coffee the last time I saw Dana alive, he had almost reached his car when he turned around and asked if I had talked to our friend lately. With a bit of an attitude, I replied, "No, Dana, I haven't." He went on and on about how if God never gives up on us, I shouldn't give up on our friend and blah, blah, blah.

I assured him I hadn't given up on him, but I was done reaching out. God is always knocking on the door of our hearts, yes, but we have to answer. I felt like I had knocked and knocked and this person wasn't answering so now I was done. I ended my rant with a promise to Dana, not knowing that would be the last time I would ever see him alive: "If he ever calls me, I promise you I'll take that call."

That night on my sofa, I was reminded of that friend. While I was still grieving Dana, I discovered it was so much more than that. These two had been two of my very best friends, like brothers, since I was five years old. With one of them off the grid and the other dead, I realized that the day Dana died, a part of me had died as well. I thought those boys would be with me for the rest of my life.

I had unforgiveness in my heart. One died, but the other left voluntarily. While I have lots of other friends, the loss of those two left me feeling very alone. I spent the better part of an hour sobbing and praying for this friend and asking God to forgive me for being so angry. Just before my sofa moment ended, I felt the Holy Spirit whisper, "He'll come around. Give him time."

Whether the cause for my anxiety attacks was self-inflicted or a direct result of "life stuff" wasn't important to me. Either way, there were things to battle on both ends. I didn't want to focus on *why* it was happening; I just wanted to deal with the root of it so that I could move forward.

And we know that God causes everything to work together for the good of those who love God and are called according to his purpose for them.

~ Romans 8:28

If that verse is true, then something good was going to come out of all of this.

Super Bowl 2012, I got a phone call. As promised, it was my friend. It had been five years since we last talked. To this day, his friendship means more to me than he may ever know.

Believe it or not, that wasn't the end of my anxiety attacks. The battle raged on.

CHAPTER THREE

I think that the most important thing a woman can have – next to talent, of course – is her hairdresser.

~ Joan Crawford

"There's nothing wrong with you." "It's all in your head." "It's just your anxiety." "You have to get a grip and stop worrying so much." These are a few of the things that were said to me when I noticed my hair was getting thin. It was May 2012. I had just got out of the shower, and my scalp caught my eye. I looked a little closer, and my heart started pounding. Is my hair getting thin?

I called a friend who is a hair stylist and asked if I could text a picture of my hair. I wanted her to tell me if it looked thin. She told me it was probably just my anxiety, and it didn't matter what she said to me because I was only going to believe what I wanted to anyways. (Thanks) I called another friend who told me I needed to get a grip and stop finding things wrong with myself. (Again, thanks)

At this point, I had been battling anxiety for about a year, and some of the people closest to me were clearly sick of me talking about it. I can't blame them. It probably would have annoyed me too, but I felt like I couldn't talk to anybody. That feeling of being all alone began to creep in again. I began to question my sanity. The line between reality and anxiety had become so completely unrecognizable that I thought I was going crazy.

After my regular doctor couldn't find anything wrong with me, I jumped online to look for a dermatologist who would hopefully confirm that I had lost my mind and I was just fine.

I was immediately diagnosed with an autoimmune disease that runs amuck in your body until all your hair is gone. There's nothing I did to contract the disease, and there is no explanation for why some people get it, and others don't. "It's just one of those things"...which made my anxiety worse in some ways.

This dermatologist told me no amount of vitamins or diet changes would cure it. There's absolutely nothing I can do but go home and wait for all my hair to fall out...but before I left she told me to buy her personal brand of shampoo. She was very rushed in her speech and said she wanted to start treatment immediately to slow the process down, not cure it, but slow it down.

She didn't tell me to go home and think about it. She didn't ask me to get a second opinion and offered no time for me to ask any questions. She wrote me up a prescription for her shampoo and set me up with another appointment for a scalp biopsy.

Since I wasn't born yesterday, I walked out of her office (without her shampoo) and started to look for a new dermatologist. I never saw her again.

When I called to make an appointment with another dermatologist I found, they said he was booked up for months. I could wait to see him or get in right away with a different doctor who was new to the practice. I think he was fresh out of school. That's not what I wanted, but I didn't feel weird about it either, so I made the appointment.

This experience was very different. In the forms I filled out, I mentioned I thought my hair loss was related to stress brought on by the death of a friend as well as the anxiety attacks I had been experiencing. As I sat in the room and waited for the doctor to come in, I felt the Holy Spirit say to me, "I want you to do the biopsy."

I sat there, quiet, and still for a moment. Finally, I just nodded my head and said to myself, "Okay, whatever tests he wants to run, just go with it. Don't overthink it.

Don't ask questions. Just go with it." I felt an absolute peace about this guy before he even walked into the room.

When the doctor came in the first thing out of his mouth was, "I'm so sorry about your friend. Can you tell me more about him and what your life was like around the time that he died?" I burst into tears. The fact that he cared enough to ask meant so much to me. At this point, I needed a good listener. He was interested in everything right down to what vitamins I was taking.

He gave me the same diagnosis as the first dermatologist. He even called in another doctor to confirm what he thought it was. Based on the timeline I gave them, they said it was the fastest progression of this particular disease they had ever seen. (Great)

As I expected, he told me he wanted to do a scalp biopsy to confirm that diagnosis. It sounds horrible, right, but I had already determined to go with whatever they wanted to do. I didn't fight it or ask any of the nervous questions that one might, under those circumstances, I simply surrendered to the process. He then said he wanted to start me on a high dose of prednisone. I never had a problem with that drug before, so I agreed to take it.

He also told me I could keep doing what I'm doing where the first doctor told me it wasn't going to help. "There's nothing wrong with vitamins."

A close friend at the time told me, "I think God allowed this to happen to you because He knew He could trust you with it." I know, right! What a weird thing to say! And what does that even mean? It sounds so heavy and feels like a lot of unwanted responsibility is attached to a statement like that.

While I never had an issue with prednisone in the past, this was a very high dose, and it was making me overly emotional and completely irrational. About one week into the prednisone treatment, I found myself in my car outside the doctor's office sobbing waiting for the office to open. When they finally opened, the doctor asked me what was wrong. Through hysterical crying, I responded with, "I don't know." You want to talk about a scary feeling? I was terrified.

Even though the experience with the second dermatologist was so much better than the first, it was hard to rid my mind of the words that the first doctor spoke to me.

(Internal Dialogue) "There's nothing you can do. Your vitamins aren't going to help. You will eventually lose all your hair, and there's nothing you can do to stop it."

One day after work, while those words were running through my mind, I slowly began to feel off. I felt light-headed, my heart started beating abnormally fast, or at least that's how it felt. I crawled into bed and called my friend Kate. Kate has been my friend since 1993, so we have a history. After about 5 minutes of me verbally throwing up on her in an anxiety-ridden state, Kate broke into prayer cutting right through my hysterical rant. I started crying. It was then I realized I hadn't cried about this yet. There I go bottling up my feelings again instead of letting them out.

When I got off the phone with Kate, I continued sobbing; about Dana, my hair, being single. As the minutes passed, I felt a peace fall over me. My heart slowed down, and anxiety lifted. I put on some music and didn't leave my bed for the rest of the night.

What music did I put on? I'm glad you asked. The song was "Human," by The Human League. (Insert your laughter here. I don't care. I love this song) I can't tell you why it works other than the nostalgic feeling I get when I hear it.

Another anxiety reliever for me is the album *Abbey Road* by The Beatles; particularly the songs, "Because" and "Sun King." That whole album is medicine to my anxiety. Other songs that calm me down without fail: "Learning to Fly" by Pink Floyd, "Silent Lucidity" by Queensryche and "Wind of Change" by Scorpions. Music would become a key player in relieving me of anxiety symptoms.

Later that month, I was in Minnesota for my annual trip to the Minnesota State Fair. And let me just say this: if you've never been, put it on your to-do list. It's the best state fair in the country. While I was there, I made an appointment with a chiropractor that my family has been going to for years. I told my sister I made the appointment in hopes of relieving some of my anxiety symptoms. She then added that your spine is also connected to your immune system, and maybe an adjustment could help with the autoimmune disease as well.

I felt so silly filling out those forms. "I'm here because I have anxiety and a disease that's threatening to take all my hair. Is there an adjustment for that?" It all sounded so crazy, but I was at the point where I was going to try everything I possibly could to fix these issues.

He gave me a standard adjustment and then said he wanted to see where my immune system was. I laid flat on my back and raised one leg in the air. He was going to push on the elevated leg as hard as he could. He said anybody with a healthy immune system should be able to keep their leg in the air, no problem.

He pushed on my leg, and it immediately fell to the table. I couldn't keep my leg up for even a couple of seconds. We tried it a second time with the same results.

Awesome Chiropractor: You have no immune system

Me: I know!

Confirming that my immune system was on vacation, he then said he wanted to drain my adrenal glands. Getting rid of all the toxins and whatever gunk is there was supposed to sort of jump start my immune system.

Awesome Chiropractor: I want you to breathe because this is really going to hurt.

Me: Good one.

Awesome Chiropractor: I'm not joking.

Me: Oh.

He was right. It was excruciating. One at a time for what seemed like five solid minutes, using his hands, he squeezed my adrenal glands. It hurt so bad it was hard to lie still. When the procedure was over, we went back to the immune system test. With one leg in the air, he pushed on it as hard as he could, and it didn't budge. He then looked at me and said, "Your immune system is back." Just like that.

Of all the doctor appointments I had over the last few months, and all the blood that was taken nobody ever told me about something as simple as getting my adrenal glands drained.

While in Minnesota, I started facing a fearful possibility...wigs. Even though my faith is strong, it's still easy to get wrapped up in the facts that were being presented to me. I decided instead of sitting in the fearful thought of if or when I would ever need a wig, I would instead conquer that fear by facing it.

I only had one friend at that time that had seen the damage this disease did to my hair, so I felt comfortable having her with me and trusted her opinion. When I got back to Arizona, we went to the recommended place and tried on different hair extensions. It was actually a lot of fun, and they looked great. I never did buy anything, but facing that fear removed it, and from that day forward, I never had any anxiety attacks brought on by thoughts about hair loss.

While it's not always that simple, sometimes the things that cause us anxiety can simply be cured by facing that fear. This was one of those things. I'm so glad instead of sitting in that fear; I instead chose to face it.

I wasn't at a point where I needed to embrace wigs, but I did have some challenges in styling my hair with the problems it was presenting. I had some bald spots the size of a dime scattered on the top of my head as well as some significant hair loss behind my ears. It looked pretty scary when my hair was wet. For over a year now, I was wearing scarves and headbands that would hide it. But those didn't make me feel attractive at all.

My hair at this point was down to my shoulders and curly. It was exhausting covering it up every single day. I didn't feel beautiful either. I felt lazy and unattractive. I'm not even sure anybody would have noticed it. Our physical flaws are always magnified through our own eyes and usually not as bad as we think.

I remember waking up one Sunday morning, and before I even opened my eyes, my internal dialogue was screaming at me.

(Internal Dialogue): "Why don't you just give up? You have too many things working against you. Nobody is ever going to ask you out now."

In spite of that, I did get up and go to church that morning, but it was with heaviness in my heart. At that moment I believed that voice I heard.

When I got to church, I was walking toward the bathroom before service when my friend Pastor Cynthia said, "Hi Stephanie! You look absolutely beautiful today. I don't know what it is but you're glowing!" I hugged her then went into the bathroom and cried.

It never seems to come the way we think it should, but Jesus does know exactly what we need when we need it. I realized at that moment the voice I heard early that morning wasn't mine and it wasn't the truth.

I learned during this time to pay more attention to what was happening around me. I woke up that Sunday morning feeling ugly and unwanted. God knew that and placed my friend Cynthia in my path to counter that thought. I could have easily blown that off and rejected her comment. Instead, I recognized it as God speaking to me, through her.

I had a follow-up appointment with my dermatologist shortly after I got back from that summer trip to Minnesota. The doctor took one look at my scalp and said, "Huh? This is weird. Your scalp isn't nearly as red as it was the last time I saw you." (Interesting)

I had finished my intense round of prednisone, and we were discussing my next steps. The options I had to choose from were steroid shots to my scalp (nope) and a pill that they use to treat lupus patients; a pill I would take for the rest of my life. The worst of the side effects were blind spots in the eyes. And remember, none of this was for a cure. It was only to delay the inevitable.

Here's the deal, I don't like to delay anything. When my boyfriend and I broke up, it was get him and his stuff out of my place as quickly as possible. Whenever I had to put a pet down, I would throw out all of the belongings related to said pet and immediately make plans to adopt a new one. It's not that I didn't love that pet or that I wasn't devastated when my relationship ended, but if there was no saving it, let's remove everything related to it so I can move on quicker.

That's the same way I approached this autoimmune disease. If the end result is, I lose all my hair, why am I delaying the inevitable? Let it all fall out now and let's deal with that sooner rather than later.

Here's why I love this dermatologist so much. He didn't demand an answer immediately. He actually suggested I go home and pray about it and if I decide to move forward with any of those options to give him a call. Now I don't know if this guy has any faith in his personal life, but the fact that he respected mine and considered it really meant a lot to me.

I chose not to move forward with any further treatment.

If we are thrown into the blazing furnace, the God whom we serve is able to save us. He will rescue us from your power, Your Majesty. **But even if he doesn't***, we want to make it clear to you, Your Majesty, that we will never serve your gods or worship the gold statue you have set up.*

~ Daniel 3:17-18 (boldface mine)

One of the leaders in my Singles small group at the time preached a sermon around this scripture.

"Even if he doesn't..." That verse knocked me out! Now, I am no Bible scholar, and I can already hear some of you saying, "that's not what that verse means," but that's the beauty of the Bible. A verse that means one thing can speak to you a different way depending on what you're going through and maybe give you a different perspective.

Here's what this verse did for me at this moment: I'm going to keep praying and do whatever I can in the natural to get my hair back. If God never heals this disease, if my hair never grows back, my faith in Him will not be shaken. God is still God, He still loves me, and I will continue to pursue Him (hair or no hair) as long as there is breath in my body. I will not let my hair (or lack thereof)

41

define me.   That verse helped give me a different perspective in the middle of my circumstances.

March 2013, roughly six months after my last appointment with the dermatologist, I attended a conference at a local church where the musical guest was Paul Wilbur. He closed the conference by singing several amazing songs; some that had lyrics in Hebrew. There were Israeli dancers pulling people out of their seats to dance with them up and down the aisles. It was one of the more beautiful things I had ever seen. The part of me that thinks I'm Jewish was in heaven.

At the end of the night, I found myself standing in the aisle with my eyes closed taking in every second of that beautiful music when I felt a hand on my shoulder and my friend Kate's voice in my ear. She was praying that I would be free from anxiety attacks. Something happened at that moment, and I felt it leave.

I never had another full-blown anxiety attack. I have felt minor symptoms of an attack, but since that night, I've been able to talk myself down every time a symptom arises.

In the past, and even a little today, flying isn't my favorite thing to do. My mind is always going over every possible thing that could go wrong. It's never kept me from getting on a plane, and I've never had a panic attack over it, but I do consider myself a little bit of a nervous traveler.

The day after that conference, I was on a plane to Las Vegas, but this time with no fear. At take-off, I put some music in my ears and was completely relaxed for the first time in a long time.

What music did I listen to? I'm glad you asked. The album is *Your Great Name* by Paul Wilbur; particularly the song titled "Song of Ezekiel." To this day, it's my traveling music. I start it up as soon as I take my seat on an airplane and I leave it on until the flight attendants start handing out drinks. That's when my nerves usually disappear.

This wasn't a pleasure trip. My brother-in-law had a booth with his company *Hold Fast Gear* at the WPPI Wedding & Portrait Photography Intl. Expo and asked if I would come and help. It's supposed to be one of the busiest photography expos, and they needed as much help as they could get.

In between checking out customers, I got a text from my then fantastic hair stylist, Erica. She said she was flipping through a magazine and found a hair restoration clinic in Mesa and thought of me. Erica also included an apology in her text saying she hopes she didn't make me feel uncomfortable for bringing it up.

Listen, for those of you who have a friend who is going through stuff (we all know somebody), and you happen to find something that could potentially help them, don't be afraid to share it; especially if it could be life-changing for them. I would never have considered a hair loss clinic if it wasn't for Erica. I'm so glad she didn't let her hesitation with how I might respond to her suggestion stop her from texting me that day.

My appointment with the hair restoration clinic was on a Thursday in June 2013; roughly ten months after my Minnesota chiropractor drained my adrenal glands. The doctor at the clinic was very friendly and gave me all the information about the different types of treatments they do. I told him about all the appointments I had over the last year with dermatologists and my primary care doctor.

I was very curious what this doctor was going to say considering the last feedback I had received regarding this "incurable disease." My Minnesota chiropractor had told me my immune system kicked back into working order, and the last thing my dermatologist said was that the redness on my scalp had significantly reduced. My hair didn't appear to be presenting any new problems since then. It hadn't started growing back in, but it wasn't getting worse either. It just sort of stopped where it was. I honestly didn't know what I was expecting this guy to say, but nothing prepared me for what he did say.

"I see absolutely no signs of an autoimmune disease." That's right. Gone!

I was shocked! It's so funny how we pray for things, we believe God hears us, yet we are shocked when He comes through. I kind of like it at the same time. I never want to lose the excitement I feel when God answers my prayers.

So the disease is gone. That's the good news. The bad news is, I am left with the damage that disease did to my scalp and hair. The hair loss clinic said they didn't want to continue treatment with me until I visited a chiropractor in Scottsdale who specialized in holistic neurological allergy testing. He wanted to get to the root of what was really going on, fix that, and then go forward with treatment to restore my hair.

I spent the next ten weeks doing allergy testing and holistic laser treatment, but I never did go back to the hair loss clinic. Those treatments are not cheap, and they are a commitment. I have reached a point where I'm comfortable with where I'm at. I don't have an urgent desire to pursue any additional treatment at this time, but I'm open to it in the future.

You're going to stop feeling sorry for yourself because I don't associate with people who blame the world for their problems. Because you're your problem, Annie, and you're also your solution.

~ Bridesmaids, the movie

It was now four years since my last relationship ended. I started to wonder if I would ever meet somebody new. All of this life stuff over the last few years had begun to eat away at my confidence, and the idea of being alone had started to settle in.

What if this was it? What if I was going to be single for the rest of my life? Will I never be able to go to a movie again? Or travel? Does that mean I'm stuck with all this crappy furniture from my early 20's for the rest of my life? And why does *alone* have to be a bad thing?

Something new was beginning to stir inside me. It had been an emotional couple of years, and I felt like I was spending too much time waiting for life to happen. Church was awesome, and I had made so many great friends there, but everybody lived a good 40 minutes from me. That left me with no real friends on my side of town.

One morning, I was craving my favorite breakfast place, and even though I battled with the idea of sitting alone in a restaurant, something took over me, and before I knew it, I was standing in the restaurant asking for a table for one. I didn't journal about this experience, so I don't remember what it was that caused the bravery to rise up in me that morning.

So what if I was alone? I sat in that restaurant by myself and had breakfast. Did it feel weird? Yes, but that doesn't mean I have to act weird. It was still early, so there were not very many people there. I brought a book with me, so it's not like I just sat there uncomfortably and looked around the room the entire time.

What else do I like to do that I have never done before alone? Could I go out alone and enjoy a movie, a concert or the Improv by myself? Perhaps it was time to find out.

Jesus said, don't worry about tomorrow. It's equally important we don't wish away today waiting for tomorrow to come.

~ Pastor Steven Furtick, Elevation Church

KISSMANIA CONCERT, 7/6/2013

I didn't journal this experience either, but I do remember it was so incredibly awkward. Attending this concert alone was very last minute. I was at a BBQ earlier that day and had a couple of friends who were planning on going with me, but slowly throughout the day every one of them backed out.

I was tired and wasn't feeling up for it myself, but one of the band members was a good friend of mine and when you have a friend in a band who "puts you on a list," you show up. What stands out about this night is the feeling of not belonging, which I would contribute to the fact that it was an evening event. Evenings feel very "date night," and I'm going alone to an event that in my mind, will be loaded with couples.

Concerts are things I want to share with people, and I discovered that night, it's not something I can easily enjoy alone. I was placed at a table with about four couples. I tried once or twice to talk to the woman next to me, but she wasn't having it.

I could have easily backed out of this show. My friend would have understood, but I want to be that friend who shows when she says she will; whether I'm alone or not. With all that said, I'm still glad I did it. I wouldn't attempt another concert alone for another five years. On New Year's Eve, 2018, I purchased one front row ticket to see pianist Jim Brickman on one of the biggest date nights of the year! Was it awkward? Not really. I have come a long way!

HARKINS THEATRES, ARIZONA MILLS MALL, GROWN UPS 2

Journal Entry 7/13/2013

I am doing it! Even as I sit here, I can't believe I am actually sitting in a movie alone. I didn't feel even a little anxiety. I thought for sure I'd sit in the back if only for the reason that no one could sit behind me and see that I'm alone. But I didn't. I sat dead center of the theatre. There are a few people behind me who, ironically, appear to be alone as well. Then there are a group of four ladies in my row sitting together.

I'm glad I came to an early movie. I'm not sure if I could ever do an evening movie alone with all the people. I bet evening movies are loaded with couples, and I think I would feel weird. I imagine it would be like that scene in Forest Gump when he was getting on the bus, and all the snotty kids kept saying to him "seats taken!"

It would be a couple of years until I went back to a movie by myself again. However, it's something I now do almost weekly by myself. This journal entry is hilarious to me because I have never felt this composed at a movie I went to alone since this day. I am awkward! I always end up in a line where I don't belong or can't seem to find which theatre I'm supposed to be in. It's pretty funny actually. It's a movie! Settle down, Stephanie!

I have several female friends who say they love going to the movies by themselves, but they're married so to me that doesn't count. Right or wrong, my perception is there's unspoken confidence that married women have.

This is how I see it: Two women, out to dinner or a movie alone. The only difference between these two women is a ring. My feeling is when somebody sees a married woman out alone, that ring tells them she's just taking a day for herself. If they see a single woman out alone (no ring) it's because she couldn't find somebody to go out with her.

There could be some truth to this, or it could be a completely irrational thought rooted in insecurity on my part. Either way, it's something I had to learn to get over. I would guess that most people aren't paying attention to the people around them. I know when I go out with friends I don't pay attention to things like that.

I eventually worked through those feelings, and now I can enjoy a movie by myself without fear of what other people might be thinking about me. I discovered bringing a book always relieves the anxiety of being alone in public. If I have my nose in a book before the movie starts, it makes it more about my time and less about everybody else around me.

TEMPE IMPROV

Journal Entry 7/19/2013

I arrived about 30 minutes early for doors to open. Not unusual for me to be ungodly early. There was one other lady in front of me at the box office. She paused, turned to me, and said, "You can go ahead of me," I said, "Thanks, but I already have my ticket." She hesitated for a minute, turned to the box office window, cleared her throat, and quietly said: "Uhm, my name is under Phoenix Singles."

OH MY GOSH! Did I seriously show up on a night when a singles group was here?? This is awesome! What stood out for me was how uncomfortable she was to say she was with a singles group.

What is this "thing" that attaches itself to a single woman and makes her feel less-than-human for being a part of a singles group or makes her think she can't be seen enjoying life in public by herself?

I learned today you have to be ready for people to pity you. Intentional or not, some of them will. It turns out this singles group was being seated right in front of me. I'm the only party of one here so far. I had a chat with my waitress for about one hour before the show started.

"Do you get very many parties of one here?"

"Yes, all the time!"

"Women?"

"Oh no, never women."

"Why do you think that is?"

It just so happened she was talking about this very thing the other day with a friend, and he told her he thinks women don't go out alone because they don't want to pay. I think that's debatable. While there are plenty of cheap, lazy women out there, I doubt that's the reason most of us don't go out alone. She told me she believed it was a lack of confidence which I completely agree with.

This ended up being the first of multiple times I would go to the Improv by myself. I LOVE the Improv! It's my happy place! If I can't find somebody to go with which I usually can't because it's not a cheap night out, I'm glad I enjoy it enough to go alone. There have been times where I don't even think to ask anybody. I just buy a ticket and go.

I've mastered it too. I am always one of the first people there, and I ask to be seated at the back wall where there is single seating facing the stage. This prevents me from being seated with groups of people and having forced conversation with strangers (which I hate) on another "date night" type event.

This is also another great place to bring a book if you're out alone; especially if you're not interested in talking to people and by people, I mean drunk men. I have had some amazing conversations with some of the people around me at the Improv, but a book helps keep the nonsense away.

Peter: I'd like to grab some dinner, please.

Waiter: Okay great, is your wife going to meet you

Peter: No

Waiter: Girlfriend?

Peter: I don't have a girlfriend.

Waiter: You just by yourself?

Peter: Yeah.

Waiter: That sucks. Do you want a magazine or something?

from the movie, Forgetting Sarah Marshall

DINNER ALONE, my 35th birthday, On The Border

Journal Entry 7/23/2013

Here I go again! The chips and salsa are all mine! And I'm getting something new. I always get the tres enchiladas. Today I'm getting the burrito with slow pulled chicken. I'm not going to lie; not having to share this salsa is pretty amazing. And the giant mango margarita has just arrived.

I still don't know how this book is going to come together. (I love that I wrote that in my journal and here I am, four years later and I'm actually writing it!! Anyways, back to my journal.)

After I got my food, about five/ten minutes had passed, and I began to feel weird. Like everybody was looking at me. Ironically I was practically alone on my side of the restaurant. I saw no one in front of me and only heard one group of two or three in the booth behind me.

I keep fidgeting with my phone or attempting to read my book, but it's not an easy task with all the food. I almost feel like I'm not supposed to be here. It's as if I'm waiting for the waitress to politely ask me to leave because I'm disturbing the other guests. Of course, I also recognize that it is all in my head and there's nothing intrusive about me having dinner by myself. Oh, the lies that can go through our heads.

I did notice a couple of things: The waitress didn't read me the specials and didn't ask me if I wanted dessert. I heard her do both of those things to the people dining around me.

Earlier, I texted two friends about my plan for a birthday dinner alone: One said, "Sweet! I love it!" and the other said, "Are you sure you wouldn't rather go with your friends?" I had a moment where I thought, wait, can I do this? Am I not supposed to have dinner alone? I quickly said to myself, no! I can go out to eat any other night. Why not on my birthday? I had no other offers for this night, but I did have a gift card from my mom and who doesn't want free Mexican food on their birthday?

Looking back, what I learned from eating dinner alone is that I don't like eating dinner alone. I'm cool with breakfast and lunch alone (which I now do often), but not dinner. Once again, it feels like "date night." I know people that love going to dinner alone. I'm not one of them, but at least I can say I tried it.

At this time in my life, I was pretty alone on my side of town. The whole point to this dinner-for-one on my birthday was that I wasn't going to sit around and wait to see if somebody offered to go out with me. Awkwardness aside, I'm so glad I did it. Since then, I've enjoyed several breakfasts and lunches out alone with little to no insecurity.

Remember KISSMANIA a few pages back? Well, it was toward the end of summer 2013 when my friend Kristine called me to tell me about a conversation she had with her husband, Mark. Mark is my friend who was a member of that band.

Mark: What's up with Stephanie?

Kristine: What do you mean?

Mark: Well, she isn't dating anybody, she came to my show alone, and she's talking about writing some book on being single. Has she completely given up on men?

Kristine (laughing): No. She just isn't putting up with the garbage anymore.

I laughed so hard when Kristine told me about this conversation. What I love about it is that there wasn't pity in Mark's voice. He just wanted to know what was up. It was an odd summer branching out and trying things on my own, but it was also the beginning of so much more. I was starting to throw out the old delusional idea that life began at marriage and stepping into a new life where I enjoy it now!

December 2013

Beauty is how you feel inside, and it reflects in your eyes. It's not something physical.

~ Sophia Loren

I was getting ready for work one morning when I felt "it's time to cut your hair." It doesn't sound like a big deal, but some people are weird about short hair on women. I mentioned it to a few acquaintances that made sure I was aware that "men don't like women with short hair." I should have known better taking that to anybody who wasn't in my inner circle of friends. And who did they think they were speaking on behalf of all men?

Why cut my hair short? I had curly hair down to my shoulders and small spots on top of my scalp that were bald. If my hair were short, I would think it would take the pressure off of my existing hair. It's just a theory. Even though it wasn't presenting any new problems, maybe I could save what hair I had by cutting it short.

At the time, my hair stylist was a super cool gal named Erica (the same Erica who recommended the hair loss clinic). I told her I had no idea what style would work with the hair loss I had, but she was free to do whatever she wanted. I could tell she was nervous not having a real plan. She was just about to start cutting when she paused and said, "You know what? Can we pray before we start?" Absolutely!

After a quick prayer and she said, "I'm just going to start and see what happens." About a quarter of the way through she shouted, "I got it! I got it! Okay, this is going to be cute!"

And it was. She gave me a short, edgy cut that I rocked for quite a few years. It evolved over time but covered what loss I did have perfectly. No more scarves or headbands. I felt beautiful again.

Shortly after cutting my hair, a male friend stopped me at church. "I need to tell you something, and I don't want you to take this the wrong way so please hear me out." Bracing myself for the worst, he continued, "I don't like short hair on women. (Yeah, yeah get on with it) In my opinion, there are only two women who can pull off short hair: Halle Berry and you. You look beautiful in short hair."

He will never know the impact those words had on me. Cutting my hair wasn't an easy decision. I had peace about it, but that didn't stop my internal dialogue from harassing me.

(Internal Dialogue) "What man is going to want a woman with short hair? Nobody is ever going to ask you out with that short, boy hair you have. Whatever sex appeal you had before is completely gone now."

I've always been insecure about the way I looked. Any new imperfection just made an already distorted self-image worse. One friend who meant well said to me, "Stephanie, everybody has something they don't like about themselves physically."

Here's why that statement fell on deaf ears. I had been battling something I don't like about myself since birth. I was born with a cleft lip. Between regular doctors' visits and being verbally tortured by kids at school and church, I spent the better part of my childhood feeling like a science experiment. I felt like I had already been dealt the *one thing* that I can't fix. Having two physical flaws that I can't control seemed unfair and cruel.

It turns out that, just like Rudolph (the red-nosed reindeer), what I initially considered to be such a negative is, in fact, the very thing that has made me stand out. Not to sound preachy, but accepting my voice has given me the confidence I've needed to pursue my dreams. And just like Seal rocks his facial scars, Cindy Crawford works her mole, and Barbra Streisand wins every race by a nose, I hope you're inspired to make the most of your possibly less-than-perfect trademark, too.

~ Ross Mathews, from his book, Man Up! Takes of my delusional self-confidence

I cried when I first read that. It inspired me to embrace my imperfections. If somebody can't see past these things that are entirely out of my control, then I don't want those people in my life. Fix what you can and make peace with what you can't.

CHAPTER FOUR

It is not our abilities that show what we truly are. It is our choices.

~ Dumbledore, Harry Potter and the Chamber of Secrets

Have you ever heard the saying, *you have to love what you do*? I'm not a big believer in that statement. I do think you should *like* what you do as long as it enables you to do what you love.

By January 2014, I was no longer just a regular usher and greeter at my church. I was doing some voluntary admin work for one of the lead pastor's assistants. I was managing book tables for special speakers, and I even had keys to the church. I was really good at it, but I wasn't passionate about it at all. Since it was a volunteer position, I never really considered doing anything different. I just liked helping.

My best friend Kate, who was also a regular volunteer, was offered a full-time position at the church. I'll never forget the look on her face when she told me. I was so happy for her, but I was also jealous; not about the job offer, but the enthusiasm she had for the job. I wasn't enthusiastic about ushering and greeting. I wanted to feel that same excitement about what I was doing.

I decided to make a major volunteer change at church; this time pointed in the direction of my heart's desire since birth. I wanted in on the production side of things.

For as long as I can remember, I have loved all things, television, and film. I wasn't the kid who went to camp in the summer. My summers consisted of me waking up early in the morning, making homemade pancakes for my two younger sisters and then taking a pen to the TV Guide to see what shows I would watch throughout the day.

Throughout my teenage years, I had accumulated a large collection of movie and TV memorabilia. I had several posters from The Three Stooges to The Blues Brothers, books about every actor imaginable including a dozen or so on Lucille Ball, hundreds of movies, lunch boxes, little figurines of The Marx Brothers and an amazing statue of W.C. Fields that my dad gave me (that still sits on my kitchen counter to this day). I even had a director's chair and a desk lamp in the shape of a movie camera. I was obsessed with everything TV and movies!

One of my senior pictures from high school was me sitting in my director's chair, surrounded by all this stuff I had collected over the years. When I was in high school, Suncoast Motion Picture Company was my FAVORITE store in the mall!

I never wanted to be an actress. I still don't. It wasn't until the winter of 2000 that I realized this was more than just a love of television and film. I had a passion for it.

The movie that changed my life was *Man on the Moon*, starring Jim Carrey. I was watching the behind the scenes of this incredible film, and something started stirring inside of me. I didn't just want to watch movies; I want to make them. I want to be *involved* in behind the scenes; not watch it at home on DVD.

It seemed like an unreachable dream for a girl living in a small town in Minnesota. Not just to me, but to a lot of people I shared that dream with. I remember one person saying to me, "What makes you so special that you think you can do that for a living? Do you know how many people try to break into that field every year and fail? You have a good job. Why don't you climb that corporate ladder and stick with something that isn't so risky."

I began a career in insurance when I was 20 years old only because I had no interest in going to college. I started in the mailroom and then moved into data entry. Almost three years into that job, I was laid off when the company was bought out but not before they sent me to Michigan for two weeks to train my replacements. Which by the way, I was completely against until my boss told me it would look really good on a resume. I reluctantly agreed. I must have left an impression on them because the Michigan office ended up offering me a job.

It was January 2002. I had a decision to make. I could take the job offer in Michigan (cold weather), find a new job in Minnesota (colder weather) or move to Arizona where three of my friends had moved just a few months earlier. I opted for warmer weather, packed up, and moved to Arizona. It was a pretty gutsy move for a 23-year-old.

It took me four months, but I did land a job with an insurance company in Scottsdale in April 2002. It ended up being a very stable job for me because I'm still working there today as an Operations Analyst, but the love for film and television never left my heart.

I'll never forget the morning that fire inside me started turning again. It was 2005. I was at work with my little clock radio tuned into a local morning show when I thought I heard the radio host say "Ron Howard." I put my ear to the radio for a closer listen, but I didn't hear him say his name a second time.

I don't know what possessed me, but I picked up the phone and called the radio station. Busy. I called a second time. Busy. I said a quick prayer under my breath, "God, I need to get through." I called a third time. This time the station answered. (What am I doing?)

Me: Hi, did I hear you say something about Ron Howard?

Radio guy: Yes, he will be a guest on our show tomorrow morning.

Ron Howard is one of my favorites! I mean, from the days of *The Andy Griffith Show* and *Happy Days* to *Parenthood* and *Apollo 13*...I LOVE RON HOWARD!

Me: Oh, cool! He is one of my favorite directors! It seems like he is one of the few people in Hollywood you can't say one bad word about. Could you tell him that a girl in Arizona thinks he is the greatest?

Radio guy: Tell you what, why don't you tell him yourself.

Oh.My.Gosh! He gave me his number and a time to call back the next day. It would be a pre-recorded question that they would play back during the interview, so I didn't get to talk directly to him, but he still got to hear my voice. The version I heard on the radio was very different from the version I recorded alone with the radio guy. It went something like this.

Radio guy: Go ahead, Stephanie.

Me: Hi. I have more of a statement than a question. I admire you as an actor, but I look up to you as a director...

Radio guy (interrupted): Are you going to school for something in film production?

Me: No, but I would love someday to be involved in the production side of making a movie.

Radio guy: What do you think, Ron? Would you hire her?

(At this point my head exploded)

Ron Howard: Well, stranger things have happened. You would be surprised at the connections I've made over the years, so if our paths happen to cross one day, remind me of this conversation, and we'll talk.

You could say this is one of the most random things that have ever happened to me, but I can't call this random. I think it was God that placed that urgency in my heart to call the radio station that morning. That conversation with Mr. Ron Howard reignited a dimly lit fire inside me. I had no idea how, where, or when, but I knew at some point, I had to find a way to get involved in this field.

It would be another nine years before I finally stepped out and took a chance on something I had absolutely no experience with; which brings us back to my volunteering at church in 2014.

Siobhan and I became friends through the singles group at church. On top of being a fantastic speaker and friend, Siobhan is on staff at church in the media department. I told her I wanted to make a switch to media and asked if she could help me with that. There were so many different opportunities to get involved in media, and with no experience, I wasn't even sure where to begin.

Siobhan started by introducing me to Dennis, the video director. I still remember the feeling I had when I walked into that control room. My knees almost buckled. I felt so much excitement looking at the screens, the racks of video equipment and the camera switcher. There were so many buttons! I wonder what they all did.

Since I didn't know what would be a good fit for me, I decided early on that whatever Dennis asked me to do, no matter how scared I felt, I would do it.

I spent the first four months observing from the control room. Whenever there was a service, I was there watching Dennis cut cameras and give direction to the camera operators. After a couple of months, I figured out some of it on my own. I usually waited until after service to ask a couple of questions to fill in the parts I couldn't figure out.

It was a Wednesday, April 2014. I was sitting in Siobhan's office talking when Dennis walked in, one hour before service and asked, "How do you feel about doing some actual work tonight? I need a camera operator."

Okay, remember when I said I set my mind that I would do whatever he asked me to no matter how scared I was? Everything inside me screamed, "NO! Say NO! You're unqualified! You've never run a camera before!"

Before my true feelings could surface, out of my mouth came, "Sure!" (What am I doing?)

He took me down to the auditorium and introduced me to Camera 2. This camera does pushes and pulls during worship and gives a head to toe shot during the sermon. I had roughly half an hour to practice before service started. I still remember hearing the countdown in my ear, and just like that, I was live.

It was a little rough but not bad for a rookie. I must not have been too bad because a week later I was asked to cover Camera 2 for all three Easter weekend services including a sketch the drama department would be putting on. I've operated a camera for one service, and now I have to shoot a drama.

I remember that drama so clearly, not because it was good, but because of what Dennis said to me over headset during service.

There was no rehearsal. There were four couples on stage. I covered the second couple and then at some point, had to pop over to the fourth couple. During the first drama, I had the second couple in my shot. Dennis cut to camera one, I swung my camera over to the fourth couple

61

and quickly adjusted my focus, and Dennis then cut to my camera and yelled over the headset, "Excellent Stephanie!"

Let me tell you. I rode that "Excellent Stephanie" high for about four weeks, and here's why: I stepped out blindly into something I was passionate about but had no known skill for. I didn't know if I would be good at anything they asked me to do. I just knew I had to try. The voices from years earlier telling me that I was nobody special to think I could ever break into this field began to fade away.

If God gives you a passion for something, He has also anointed you with the ability to do it. You just have to step out. If this is what God wants me to do, he will open the door for me to do it, but it wasn't going to happen on its own magically. I had to move my feet first. And what do you know? I was actually good at it.

Like most things, some services were better than others, but the more I ran those cameras, the better I got. Before you knew it, I had been moved over to Camera 1, which is a tight, elbows-up shot and usually the one that is live to the side screens for most of the service. It takes a lot more concentration to run that camera.

I was a camera operator for a full year. When I wasn't scheduled, I sat in the control room and watched. Eventually, Dennis gave me a quick lesson in engineering, which is adjusting the brightness, contrast, and color control of the individual camera shots. Dennis usually directed and engineered himself so by teaching me, at least I was helping him instead of just sitting in the control room watching.

This also opened the door to paid camera jobs. If there was a graduation or a conference that required media, I was always asked if I would run a camera. It made my life pretty hectic. Remember, I was working a full-time job, volunteering at church every single service; Wednesday night, Saturday night and both services Sunday, as well as several Friday night high school or college graduations leaving me with very little if any, alone time or time with my friends. It was basically free schooling, so it was a sacrifice I was willing to make. I would be stupid not to take full advantage of that.

One day, one of the Camera 4 operators asked me when I was going to run Camera 4. This is a multi-axis control camera that is on a 24' long arm and swings out over the congregation and creates fluid motion gliding shots. There are a lot of moving parts to this camera, so it was intimidating for sure. He told me only one other woman has ever run that camera before, and for some reason, he thought I could run it.

In between services, I went down to the platform that Camera 4 was on, and he went over all the moving parts with me. I would mess around with it every couple of weeks and try to get a feel for it, but I never did get to run that camera during a service. I guess God had other plans for me.

****

In the summer of 2014, during my annual trip to Minnesota, I was sitting in my niece's bedroom with my sister Melinda folding laundry and listening to James Taylor; she has his best of album playing on a loop in her daughter's bedroom.

For the last several years, Melinda had been tossing around the idea of getting matching tattoos. I honestly never thought I would find something that I would ever want to place on my body permanently, so I never took it that seriously. It was just something we talked about. If I actually go through with getting a tattoo, it has to mean something to me. I won't do it unless it hits my heart.

I certainly never considered getting one before I was married. I had somehow decided it would ruin my wedding photos if I had a visible tattoo. At this point, I was 36 years old and single with absolutely no prospects.

And then it happened. The song "Secret O' Life" started playing. *Try not to try too hard; it's just a lovely ride.* I had posted those words to Facebook a couple of times over the years. I always loved that song. My sister and I started talking about the first memory we have of hearing that song. It was when James Taylor performed it on *Saturday Night Live* in the 1990s. We were captivated by those lyrics.

I sat there for a moment and listened to the song, tears began to well up in my eyes, and I said, "That's it! That's the tattoo! *Try not to try too hard; it's just a lovely ride.*"

November 15, 2014 (coincidentally, four years to the date that my friend Dana died), I got that tattoo on the inside of my forearm. A few months later, my sister got those same lyrics on her shoulder blade. I can't tell you how many times I've looked down at my arm and was reminded, in a moment of anxiety or worry, to relax, stop taking myself so seriously and just enjoy the ride.

****

My commute from home to church at this time was roughly forty minutes one way. Once I started getting my feet wet and realized I was going to fully commit to volunteering in the media department, I knew I had to

64

move closer to church. December was fast approaching, and our Christmas production would soon be in full swing.

The Christmas production is a Broadway-style show, fifteen shows over ten straight days all while working a full-time job. The past few years as an usher and greeter, my schedule was rough but manageable. I had a 25-minute drive to work and had to be there by 6:30 am.

At 2:30 pm, when I was off work, I would go pick something up for dinner and drive another 20 minutes to church where I would just hang out until the 5:30 pm meeting before the doors opened. I volunteered from 5:30 pm to roughly 8 pm for every show and would then start my 40-minute drive home. I was usually in bed between 9:30 and 10 pm and would be up again at 4:30 am for work the next day. I did this for ten days, every December for three years.

Now that I was in the media department, my time commitment was going to be much more rigorous than when I was an usher. It would involve camera rehearsals, dress rehearsals, tech rehearsals, and I would have to stay for the entire show. There is no leaving halfway through for camera crew.

I moved to North Phoenix in November 2014 but not before I got rid of all the old furniture I had from my 20's. The only piece of furniture I took with me was a new sofa I had purchased earlier that year. My entertainment center, kitchen table, patio furniture, and my bed either got tossed or picked up by Salvation Army.

It felt so good to get rid of all that old furniture. I kept telling myself I would get new furniture after I'm married. There is no sense in getting new stuff now. I'll happily hang on to my old, crappy things until I marry into some new furniture. I was tired of waiting for marriage to have nice things. It might take me some time, but I was going to buy some new furniture and tossing out the old was the best way to encourage me to replace it.

Moving to Phoenix meant no more 40-minute commute to church or 25-minute commute to work. I was now living 3 miles from church and 7 miles from work, so I was also saving some serious money in gas. Because I had tossed my bed before the move, I spent my first three months in Phoenix sleeping on my sofa.

President's Day, 2015 I walked into a furniture store and left with my first bedroom set; a queen sleigh bed including box spring and mattress, one five-drawer dresser and two night stands. I had always wanted a "grown-up" bedroom set. The voice that told me it was a waste of money to have such nice things as a single woman was replaced with a voice telling me, why not now? You have the money. Give yourself the life you want and stop waiting for it to happen. I still smile when I look at that bedroom set.

While at a church event, I ran into an acquaintance I hadn't seen in a while.

"Stephanie! I haven't seen you in a long time. How are you?"

"I'm good! I'm a camera operator now during services, so that's probably why you haven't seen me around."

"I didn't know you were interested in that."

"You know what's funny? I saw Paul McCartney in concert about a week ago. Kate and I were seven rows from the stage, and all I could do was watch the camera operators."

"That's so funny! I know the video director that works at that arena. I'll have him give you a call."

He called me a week later.

What just happened?!? I'm running cameras at church, and now I have a meeting with the director at a major sports arena for a possible job running cameras during sporting events? How cool is that?! I took a tour of the arena about two weeks later. It was by far the coolest behind-the-scenes tour I've ever taken. We seemed to get along great, and he told me he would call me in a week or so.

No phone call.

I followed up two weeks later, but he didn't return my call. I gave it one more week and followed up with an email. I got one response saying he's been really busy, but he will get back to me as soon as he can.

I ran into my friend a few weeks later, and she urged me to follow up with him one more time. She said he has a lot going on, but he's interested in me. "Don't give up. Keep calling him." I called him one more time, and he never called me back. I let it go after that.

Let me tell you why this wasn't a massive disappointment for me. I believe that if God wanted me to get that job, there is nobody on earth who could keep me from it. I did my part by making the appointment and following up not twice, but three times over two months and he never called me back. Plus, who wants to work for somebody who's that flaky? I know I don't.

I was bummed for sure. It sounded like an awesome opportunity, but if God doesn't want me there, then He must have something else in mind. Why did He allow that opportunity to cross my path if it wasn't what He wanted for me? I'm glad you asked. I look at these failed opportunities as little glimpses into what *could be*. I imagine God saying, "Hey, I haven't forgotten about you. That isn't where I want you, but if you think that was cool, wait until you see what I have over here for you."

If God allowed an opportunity like that to pass by me, what did He have waiting for me down the road?

Just one month before this conversation, I received a phone call from a friend who said he had a dream about me. In this dream, he was visiting me at a Hollywood studio. He said I was working on a documentary with Ron Howard.

Let me stop here for a moment; at the time I got this phone call, Ron Howard was working on a documentary for Hulu on The Beatles. My favorite director, and my favorite band together. That alone made my head explode, and now my friend is having a dream about me working with him.

Back to his dream, he said he never saw me there, but my assistant gave him a tour of the studio and was telling him about all my accomplishments since my script was discovered and that he saw a director's chair with my name on it. He ended by saying, "That's it. I don't know what it means, but I'd pray about it if I were you. Talk to you later." (click)

I just sat there with my cell phone in my hand and a blank look on my face. Did I also mention that only two days before this phone call I had taken my dusty director's chair out of my bedroom closet and placed it in my living room? I'm not making that up. That actually happened.

The next night I had a dream that I was at a party with Jerry Mathers and Ken Osmond (from the show *Leave It to Beaver*). I remember saying, "Hi Ken!" and we gave each other a big hug. Jerry hugged me and said, "Tony (Dow) is on his way."

A few weeks later, Roma Downy and Mark Burnett were at church talking about their upcoming miniseries, *The Bible*. I begged Dennis to keep me off the schedule so I could sit in the audience and listen to them speak. I got to hear maybe ten minutes when my cell phone buzzed. It was Dennis. He apologized and said he needed me upstairs in Shawn's office. (Well, at least I got to listen for a few minutes).

When I got upstairs, Dennis son, Tristan needed help setting up some camera equipment. I ran around helping him for half an hour or so when Tristan said: "Can you sit on the couch so I can check the lighting before they get here?" I said, "Before who gets here?" and in walked Mark Burnett and Roma Downy.

So now I'm sharing a very small space with one of the biggest producers in television. How did this happen?? I got to monitor the sound for a series of short videos we shot with them. They were both so nice.

I left that video shoot, popped my head into the control room and said: "Thank you, Dennis." He smiled and said, "I thought you'd like that."

MARCH 2015

Visions are worth fighting for. Why spend your life making someone else's dreams?

~ Tim Burton

In between Sunday services, I usually went down to the main floor and spent a couple of minutes with my friend Kate. Sometimes I would walk the hall that surrounded the sanctuary and see if I ran into anybody I knew. If I wasn't running a camera, I was up in the control room that was located in the first balcony, so I didn't see as many people as I used to when I was an usher. It was nice to make the rounds once in a while and get hugs from some familiar faces.

On one of these walks, I ran into Pastor Saeed. He was sitting in a chair. As I walked by, I said, "Hi Pastor Saeed" "Hello Director" was his reply. This wasn't the first time he had said this to me. I blew it off the first couple of times, but this time I stopped, turned to him, and asked, "Why do you keep calling me that?" He knows my name. It was weird that all of a sudden, he was calling me a director.

Saeed: You know you're a director, right?

Me: No.

Saeed: Well, you are. It's coming.

I'm not going to lie. This tripped me out a little bit. There are a lot of weird people in the world who say goofy things about what you should be doing and "the Lord sayeth this about your life" kind of stuff. It's happened to me more times than I care to discuss. But when it comes to Pastor Saeed, when that man speaks, I listen. Don't confuse that with me hanging on to every word he says. I still took those words he spoke over me to God. I went back to the control room and said a quick prayer.

"Alright God, listen, I could marry a director and help him the rest of my life and be perfectly happy, but what do YOU want me to do?"

I felt so unworthy of that title. Director? Me? I've been running cameras for a year. What made him think I could be a director? What makes me think I can't be a director? I'm not trying to play the woman card here, but I was working in a department that appeared to be a big boys club. The boys never treated me any different because I was a woman, which I love about them, and they made me work just as hard as everybody else. But the thought of directing intimidated me. I didn't say a word to

70

anybody about that conversation with Pastor Saeed. I prayed about it once, and I moved on.

Just a few weeks later, I found myself in the control room talking with Dennis on a Saturday night during rehearsal. Siobhan and I had just attended a wedding and had to come back to church to take care of a couple of things for service before going back to the reception. Then it happened.

Dennis: So, you've mastered Camera One and Camera Two. I know you've been toying around with Camera 4, but I was wondering, how do you feel about directing?

Me: Directing?

Dennis: I think you're ready.

And there it is. I got a word from Pastor Saeed, I prayed about it once, and a few weeks later, Dennis asked me to start directing. This is one of those moments where you pray about something, and when it actually comes to pass, you're still shocked it happened. Putting my life in God's hands and trusting Him to guide my steps has not always been an easy thing to do, but it sure is exciting.

I spent the remainder of 2015, focusing on directing. I still ran camera for services on occasion and was still given the paid jobs as well, but once they saw I was willing to learn and was actually pretty good at it, my name usually fell on the schedule under director.

Not long after I had settled into directing, if Dennis needed a weekend off, I was asked to cover all three-weekend services. I don't think it was that big of a deal to the media boys, they always had more faith in my ability to direct than I did in myself, but I considered it quite an honor to be given that responsibility as a rookie director. I remember one conversation I had with Shawn, who was the media supervisor at the time, during my first paid gig as a director for a youth conference.

Me: I don't feel qualified to do this.

Shawn: Technically, nobody is qualified until they start doing it.

Me: I guess.

Shawn: If I didn't think you could do it, I never would have asked you.

Being a woman in the media department did not come without challenges. No matter how great most of the men I worked with were, there is always one who has to make sure I know he could be doing what I do if he really wanted to. I've been told I'm talking too loud and too quiet during the same service. I've been criticized for the shots I took as a director and a camera operator. I even had rubber bands shot at me while directing...during a church service!

I think the biggest battle in becoming a director was choosing to believe in myself. I cared too much what Shawn and Dennis thought about me. Even though they never gave me cause to worry, I was terrified of letting them down. I found myself saying the same things that the voices of the past said to me.

(Internal Dialogue) "What makes you so special that you think you can do this?"

I eventually reached a point where any time I felt unworthy or unqualified for whatever the boys asked me to do, I remembered the words Shawn said to me. "If I didn't think you could do it, I never would have asked you." He had a significant impact on me during those years. He pushed me to be better and more importantly, to believe in myself. (Thank you, Shawn)

I tried from that day forward to not be verbal about the insecurity I was feeling. If the boys believed in me, I needed to work on believing in myself. The insecurity I was feeling wasn't their problem; it was mine.

Media women are strong. We have to be working in a boys club

~ *My friend, Siobhan*

CHAPTER FIVE

That's not a good enough offer for me. I'm not willing to gamble my whole life on somebody who's not quite sure. I'm still looking for something more extraordinary than that.

~ Bridget Jones's Diary, the movie

By 2009, I mastered what not to do in relationships. Ten years ago, my bar was pretty low. I would have found somebody I was interested in, created any and all excuses to place myself in front of him and tried my best to manufacture a relationship. If it worked, it would ultimately end in disaster and heartbreak. I was done with that approach, so I had to learn a new way.

I knew full surrender to God, and letting Him have control was the first step. I also knew I played a part in that. I just didn't know what it was. I was afraid of going back to past behavior by trying to make something happen myself. I figured if a guy were interested in me, he would ask me out and I wouldn't have to do anything to encourage that.

So what do I do in the meantime? The problem I was running into is when I saw somebody I was interested in I got so nervous I avoided them. Why? Several reasons come to mind.

First, I don't flirt, and even if I did, I am not gifted in that area and to make matters worse, I have no idea when I'm being flirted with.

During one of my trips to Minnesota, I was talking to my friend Amanda about something a guy at church said to me.

Amanda: "Stephanie! That's flirting. He's flirting with you!"

Me: "He is?!?"

Amanda: "Yes! Ugh, you're going to be single forever."

Second, I have no game. One time a cute guy at my apartment complex said hi to me, and as I said hi back, I immediately fell into a bush. That actually happened. Another time at a piano bar in San Diego, I was watching one of the piano players from across the room. (I have a thing for men who play the piano.) When his time was over, and his replacement showed up, he walked off the stage and was heading right in my direction. Did I say hi? Make eye contact? No. I immediately got nervous and looked straight at the floor as he walked by me and out of my life forever.

On some occasions, I wouldn't even acknowledge somebody I was interested in. Great, I've mastered how not to manufacture a relationship, but now he thinks I'm a bitch or at the very least, I'm sending mixed signals. I had to find a balance. I had swung so far to the other side; I was afraid I was turning everybody off.

I really did want to do things God's way, but the line between God's way and my old ways had become so blurry that it was making me obsess about my intentions.

(Internal Dialogue) "He's going to think you have a motive for saying hi to him. You're supposed to be letting a man pursue you, and here you go again pursuing him. This isn't what God wants you to do. You're supposed to be waiting on Him, and here you are going right back to your old behavior. You haven't changed at all."

Sometimes friends can make that voice scream even louder. "Ooh, are you over here hoping to run into that guy?" The comment isn't meant to be cruel. It's just innocent teasing, but comments like that bother me because all I hear is somebody questioning my intentions. In most cases, I wasn't even trying to get anybody's attention; I was simply saying hello when I walked into a room or going about my normal life when somebody decided to pick on me about somebody I was interested in.

My internal dialogue needed to stop or at the very least, lower its voice.

I had to stop obsessing. There will always be somebody who questions your intentions. I am going to make mistakes, but at the end of the day, God knows my heart. I'm not responsible for what other people might think about me.

The best advice I got was from my friend, Pastor Cynthia. She told me one day over lunch that I need to relax. "A guy can't fall in love with you if he doesn't know who you are."

I decided then to do my best to treat everybody as if they were my friend. That way everybody is getting the same authentic version of me vs. the obsessive, neurotic overthinking version (as entertaining as she can be). And quite frankly, it was so much easier than going back and forth in my mind over what was okay to say and what wasn't.

While this helps me with how I should treat men in general, it doesn't eliminate the nerd factor. That is still ever-present and rears its awkward head whenever somebody remotely attractive says hello to me.

Just last weekend at church, I was reading a book before service when I saw somebody approach me from the corner of my eye. I closed my book and turned around to see a rather handsome man standing there. He put out his hand and said,

"I don't believe we've met. What's your name?"

Caught off guard by how handsome he was, I managed to get out, "Stephanie."

"Stephanie, where are you from?"

I just sat there staring at him as I responded slowly with "Arizona." He then looked confused. Perhaps he didn't ask me that question and I just verbally puked Arizona at him because I was nervous.

"So, Phoenix or do you live in another part of town?"

"No, I don't know why I said that. I'm originally from Minnesota, but I've lived in Arizona for sixteen years."

Can you believe I actually corrected myself out loud to him! I am completely insane. I eventually relaxed, and we had a nice conversation, but it was a disaster to begin with. At least that's how I remember it.

Jenna Maroney: That guy wanted to buy you a drink.

Liz Lemon: Really? I already have a drink. Do you think he'd buy me mozzarella sticks?

~ 30 Rock, the TV show

As awkward as I can be, I will always have a good laugh about it later. I rarely beat myself up over things like this. The comedian in me finds it all very entertaining after the fact. A friend once told me she believes my man will find it endearing. I find it very entertaining myself, so there has to be a man out there who feels the same way about my lack of composure.

What I don't struggle with is how I want to be pursued.

A couple of friends at church told me the story of how they pursued their wives. They were both very similar. Both men laid out their intentions in a clear way from the beginning, so there were no misunderstandings. They both said they wanted to date with the intent of marriage.

They were open and transparent about their past and said they would answer any questions they might have. If they didn't want to move forward with a relationship based on those answers, they were free to leave. If not, their past cannot be an issue going forward. The conversation got started; they ended up dating and were eventually married.

That raised my bar for how I wanted to be pursued. I not only want, I need that kind of transparency in a relationship.

The problem that comes with raising your bar is it can give off the appearance that you're too picky. The older I get, the more I appreciate how amazing my single life is. And the more I realize what I'll be giving up, the higher that bar goes.

I don't want to be someone that anyone settles for. Marriage is hard enough without bringing such low expectations into it, isn't it?

~ from the movie, Sleepless in Seattle

I don't think that's a bad thing. Look, there are plenty of men out there I could have married by now, but I'm not looking for average. I'm looking for somebody who isn't going to screw around; somebody who wants to say "I do" and means it. A lot of people don't mean it anymore. For some, things get just a tiny bit rough, and before you know it, they're throwing around the word, divorce. Knowing that the person who says "I do" to me means it, is very important for me. I refuse to settle no matter how many people tell me I'm too picky.

78

Don't get me wrong; I don't have a script that some poor dude has to blindly try to figure out, or I won't go out with him. I have no idea how it will end up happening, but I have some things that I consider red flags. Just so we're clear, I'm not talking about character flaws. I think a red flag is a sign that points to a character flaw. This is something that I would see in a man when I first meet him or begin dating.

I have spent several years observing people; how single women treat men and more importantly, how single women treated each other. I also paid very close attention to how I was being treated. The more I fell in love with myself and discovered what my heart really needed from a man, the more quickly my bullshit detector began working, and the less tolerant I became of bad or shady behavior. Those observations taught me how I wanted to be treated and made me more intentional with how I treat other people.

Annoying exchange #1: I had a friend who I got together with once or twice a year. There is no real reason for why we didn't spend more time together; that's just the kind of friendship we had. One night, over dinner and more than six years into our friendship, he started springing these weird questions on me

"Do you ever think about me?"

"What do you mean?"

"I mean, you're one of the coolest girls I know. How come we never dated?"

(Because you never asked) "I don't know."

This went on every time I saw him for a couple of years. We still only saw each other once or twice a year. The phone call frequency never increased, and more importantly, he never one time made it clear to me what he was driving at. Which brings me to my first red flag: If he isn't direct with me.

I am 40 years old. The time for cute, flirtatious games has come and gone. When I talked to my friend, Pastor Jim about this conversation, he said, "That is a passive-aggressive way of letting you make the first move. You don't want to go out with him. He's being lazy."

Tell me what you want. I am not a mind reader. I had another guy say to me twice in one year, "I want you to know I'm praying about you." After the second time, I rolled my eyes and said to myself, "Well stop praying and make a decision!"

Another example of this is the phrase, "We should get together some time." I had one dude who would always pose this question to me with no follow-up. I think this is a lazy, noncommittal way to maintain a friendship. I interpret "We should get together sometime" as "Hey, I'm thinking about you, but to avoid inconveniencing myself, I'll send this little message that keeps you on the back burner just in case I don't have something to do one day."

I will respond to this in one of two ways: 1) "Great! What day works best for you?" This puts the ball back in their court. If they come back with a date and time, then I know they were serious. If they are weird and iffy about setting a date then I know it was nonsense and they really didn't mean it. 2) I won't respond at all. Either you want to see me, or you don't. If you want to see me, show some effort, or I will bounce.

Moving on! Annoying Exchange #2: One Sunday before service, I got a text from a male friend.

"Hey, are you at church today?"

"Yes. I'm in the control room."

"I'm on my way up."

He came up a few minutes later. I hadn't seen him in a while, so we spent a few minutes catching up. I saw on Facebook that he had a girlfriend so naturally, I asked why he didn't bring her up with him.

"Oh no, she's not my girlfriend. I don't want to put a label on it. We're just having a good time. You know you're still my number one girl."

This bullshit is my second red flag. Listen, I am not anybody's number one if there's a number two. It wasn't so much what he said but the attitude in which he said it. It's as though he expected me to fall all over him with gratitude for having given me the honor of being his number one. Gross! A guy, acting like a jerk but thinking he's God's gift to women is the quickest way to get an eye roll out of me.

First of all, let's talk about this girlfriend who he left sitting by herself so he could come flirt with me. Perhaps they did have a causal relationship. Okay, fine, but I don't do that. I would be heartbroken if I was dating a man and he was talking this way about me when I wasn't around while hitting on other women.

Next, I simply deserve better than that. I've been hurt in relationships before. I've been cheated on, lied to, taken advantage of and made a fool of so I don't have time for this kind of behavior and believe me I am ready to experience something a little more authentic.

And finally, I VALUE LOYALTY. I am a very loyal woman. It takes A LOT to get me to walk away. If I ended every relationship or friendship I had just because things got hard, I wouldn't have anybody in my life.

Don't get me wrong; I do know how to walk away. There are a small number of times in my forty years where I've had to cut ties with somebody for one reason or another because it wasn't a healthy friendship. Over time, God helped restore several of those friendships. I am always open to reconciliation. Usually, most things can be worked out as long as both people want it.

One example is my friend Scott. In 2002, I moved to Arizona with a few friends (Scott was one of them) where our friendship became rocky. In 2004, Scott moved back to Minnesota, and we had a falling out. I do not remember what circumstances surrounded our falling out (and neither does he), but I remember I had never been angrier with him than I was around that time.

In 2007, I went back home for my ten-year high school reunion. Scott and I had not spoken in three years. I was at Buffalo Wild Wings in Elk River, Minnesota, with at least ten other friends when I noticed Scott sitting at the bar. I tried to position myself in front of my friend Kate, so there was no chance of him seeing me. I had no interest in talking to him that night or any other night.

After a while, the waitress walked over and said, "There's a gentleman at the bar who would like to buy you a drink." "Is his name, Scott?" "Yes," she replied with an apprehensive look on her face. "Ugh" (as I rolled my eyes) "I'll have a White Russian." Kate whispered, "What are you doing?" I said, "Screw that guy! He can buy me drinks all night as long as he doesn't talk to me."

Then he walked over. This Scott was different. I didn't know this, Scott. He had a look of humility to him that I had never seen before. He said, "Hey, I don't want to bother you or interrupt your evening. I just want to tell you I'm sorry for destroying our friendship."

And just like that, we were friends again.

One year later, he introduced me to the woman who would become his wife. Becky quickly became one of my closest friends and still is to this day.

Scott and Becky moved to Arizona in 2018 and forever changed my social life. When the three of us are together, we laugh a lot. Scott is so incredibly funny and makes me laugh every time we are together. I think Scott really does love that Becky and I are so close, but he does give us a hard time once in a while.

Me: I don't know what I would do without you, Becky.

Scott: Hello!! What the hell?!?

Dana left a huge hole in my heart when he died. I have a few special male friendships in my life, but Scott has been a constant since that night in 2007 at Buffalo Wild Wings when our friendship was restored.

Another example is my ex-boyfriend. Do you remember the painful breakup I mentioned at the beginning of this book from 2009? He ended up moving to Dallas shortly after our breakup. I got a phone call from him in 2011 that, without getting into details, was all kinds of emotional. I told him I couldn't speak to him anymore and that trying to be friends with him was just too hard. We didn't talk for four years.

In October of 2014, I got a Facebook message from him letting me know he was coming to town and that he was open to seeing me if I wanted. I never replied to that message. It just didn't feel right.

That December during the Christmas Production at church, I found myself up at the Prayer Pavilion before every show. I had a few people on my heart at the end of 2014, and my ex-boyfriend was one of them. I spent an hour before each show praying for whatever and whoever was on my heart at that time. Maybe it's because he had messaged me a few months before, maybe it was God, who knows.

January 2015, I received a second message from him. I opened this message to find the mother of all apologies. He apologized for everything that he did wrong in our relationship, apologized for how badly he treated me and told me that he would very much like to connect again, as friends, only if I wanted. If I wasn't comfortable, he understood. He just needed me to know how sorry he was.

I immediately knew I was supposed to respond to his message, but I didn't want to open the door to my past unless God made it clear to me I was supposed to. My friend Kate was with me when I got the message, and she quickly responded with, "No, thanks! It's been real!" (I love Kate)

That same night, I read the message to my friend Siobhan, and she said, "Wow! How are you going to respond? You are going to respond, aren't you? You know you have to write him back." I said, "I know."

It didn't happen overnight, but we slowly started talking again first over text and eventually a phone conversation. One year later, he came to visit his family in Mesa, and we spent some time together. That following year I flew to Dallas to visit him. It sounds weird, right, but we are just friends. And it's a great friendship at that!

Not everybody gets it, but that's okay. I can't tell you how often I hear "You two have such great chemistry. Are you sure you don't want to get back together?" (Yes, I'm sure) Great chemistry? So what? I could have chemistry with a stranger at the grocery store. Doesn't mean I should marry him. And of course, we have great chemistry. We've known each other for twelve years.

In general, I wouldn't recommend it, but it works for us. We have rules and boundaries as any male/female friendship should. As long as we're both single, we are free to be friends, but as soon as there's a girlfriend or a boyfriend, the phone calls stop out of respect for that relationship. I never want to be the reason a relationship of his doesn't work out, and he feels the same way about me. I have nothing against having friends of the opposite sex, but when you used to date, the rules are a little different.

I'm glad I listened to that feeling that told me to respond to his message. While I forgave him a long time ago and I didn't need his apology to pray for him, it did take me to a whole new level of closure and forgiveness.

Is it normal to be friends with your exes? I don't know. I had one male friend who said, "No. I'm not okay with that. You can't be friends with your ex." To which I responded, "Well, I'm not married to you, so you don't get to tell me what's okay and what isn't." (Weirdo)

I kind of went through this in reverse with my friend Dana. I remember when I was 20-ish and my boyfriend at the time told me he wasn't sure he was comfortable with one of my best friends being a guy. I said, "Then you better get to know him because he's not going anywhere."

One night Dana had a party at his parent's house. I was getting ready to leave when my boyfriend said he was going to stay. I looked at Dana, then back to my boyfriend and said, "You're staying?" and he said yes. Dana and I exchanged a look, and I said okay and left.

The next day Dana called me and said: "Your boyfriend is weird." I said, "I know! What happened after I left?" and he said he kept asking all sorts of questions about our friendship and asked if we ever dated. Dana said, "I told him you don't date a chick you used to take a bath with when you were kids."

After that night, that boyfriend never had a problem with Dana being around. There are always two perspectives when somebody new gets introduced into an already established circle of friends. Dana wasn't a threat to me or anybody that knew him, but to a guy I just started dating, it was a concern. I can see that now that I'm older.

I have some great male friends in my life. As long as there are boundaries within those friendships (and there are) and I'm honest about the history I have with them, whoever I end up marrying shouldn't have a problem with it.

One of my ex-boyfriends ended up marrying a friend of mine, and they have two kids and live in Minnesota. Because I'm friends with his wife, they're a little more present in my life than my most recent ex-boyfriend. We see each other every couple of years when I'm in Minnesota. I make plans to see her, and if he's there, that's her choice. He is her husband now, so I let her drive that.

My most recent ex-boyfriend lives in Dallas and has been in a relationship for seven months now. As I said, we have boundaries and are respectful of any new relationships that are formed, *especially since we used to date*. It stinks that this friendship will inevitably come to an end, but we had a really nice run for the last few years where we were able to forgive each other and make better memories than the ones we had when we were dating, and for that, I will always be grateful.

My other former friendships that are still severed are for good reasons. Because I'm loyal I don't deal well with people who can write me off for stupid reasons. For example, I had one friend write me off when I moved into media at church and ended a volunteer position I was in with her. She told several people in my church that I was "disobedient to God" and that I "missed my calling."

Right! Any time somebody tries to be the Holy Spirit to you, RUN. My relationship with God is between God and me. Anybody who tries to come in and manipulate me for their own agenda, and uses God as a way to do that, isn't going to be in my life for very long.

I had friends who wrote me off because I didn't answer a phone call or a text. That actually happened. Friendships ended because of a misunderstanding. A misunderstanding that I spent months trying to get to the bottom of and once they were *finally* honest with me about it, it was too late. They had both checked out.

As painful as it was, I'm glad these "friendships" ended before things got too out of control. It's weird when your *married* girlfriends have unhealthy expectations of you and make *you* responsible for things in *their* lives that you should not be responsible for. Then you end up having to ask them, "Do you think we're dating?"

This kind of rejection is so hard for me to recover from. I have a lot of longevity in my friendships, and it wasn't until my late thirties when this nonsense started happening. I spent months crying and praying about what I could have done differently to have prevented this from happening. There had to be a common denominator somewhere in here. What is it that I'm doing that these "friends" can just bail without an adult conversation? That's right. They ended our friendship over text, like teenagers.

After months of self-evaluation and prayer, I came to the conclusion that the common denominator was both their behavior and my reaction to their behavior. In all these cases, these friendships reached a point where I was walking on eggshells with them. They voiced their disapproval of me having a life outside of them. They made terrible assumptions about me, and instead of simply calling and straightening it out, they took to social media. But where my money and my time were concerned, they had no complaints.

I realized I probably place people in my inner circle a little quicker than I should. I now take more time to get to know people before giving them that much access to my heart. These particular rejections were blessings in disguise. I was spending way too much time preparing for their reaction to my damned if I do, damned if I don't interactions with them.

Just because you're not included, doesn't mean you're being excluded.

~ Josh Wolf, from the podcast, Prinze & The Wolf

At the end of the day, it wasn't about me. Jealousy and unhealthy expectations have no place in relationships. If I get a phone call or text and that I don't want to take because I'm in the middle of a movie or I just don't feel like talking, that's my choice. I'm not married to you. (That's one of my favorite things to say) I don't have to answer my phone every time it rings.

Which brings me to this red flag: If he's a control freak. Now, I think we all have a little bit of this in our DNA in one way or another. I'm referring to an extreme kind of control. Because of lousy past friendships (like the ones you just read about) I have a low tolerance for somebody who tries to control me in ridiculously annoying ways.

Annoying Exchange #3: A friend of mine asked if he could take me out for my birthday to my favorite restaurant. In between the time we finally nailed down a date and the date itself, my favorite restaurant closed its doors. (I'm still not over it. Pool tables, dart boards, music, and they served Chinese food! You could play pool and eat an egg roll! I miss that place.) I texted him, giving him two other options for where we could meet.

He said no to both and recommended a third place.

Are you following me? He offered to take me out for *my* birthday, said no to where I wanted to go and recommended his favorite place. I was mildly annoyed but said okay and just went with it. Pick your battles.

After we went back and forth a couple of times, we finally agreed to meet at 5:30. I showed up at 5:15 (fifteen minutes early) and got a booth. He showed up at 5:45 (fifteen minutes late).

The control continued as soon as he sat down.

"I was kind of hoping to sit in the bar area by the pool tables."

"Well, I didn't know that."

"I thought we could play pool with another couple."

(We are not a couple) "You said dinner. I thought we were going to eat and catch up." Did I mention he had his face in his phone for most of this conversation?

"I should see if there's a movie we could catch after dinner." (We never discussed a movie prior to this)

"I can't go to a movie tonight. I have to work tomorrow."

"Oh, you can go to a movie." (He said with a tone that indicated I was dramatic)

Can we talk about the cell phone for a minute? I love my cell phone too, but when I'm on a date, and he can't stay off his phone, I won't go out with him again. I have been out to dinner with friends and have been the only one sitting there while everybody else had their face in their cell phone. Minutes are literally ticking by, and I'm just sitting there.

I secretly love to remedy things like this once in a while. I find it fascinating how much we miss because we cannot put our phones down. I've been guilty of it too, but in the last few years, I've made a real effort to not be on my phone when I'm with friends.

"No, I can't go to a movie. I have to work tomorrow."

Then the waitress comes over and asks what I would like to drink.

"I'll have a Heineken."

"Are you sure you don't want one of their margaritas? They have great margaritas."

"I don't want a margarita."

Now I'm just annoyed and pushing back. This is the kind of control I can't handle. He tried to change everything about that night right down to what drink I ordered. It wouldn't have been a big deal if it wasn't for him trying to change every single detail about that night.

Annoying Exchange #4: My friend Kate and I were invited to meet a male friend of ours for dinner with several of his friends. When I got there, it was almost all women. It seemed weird to me at first, but I have a lot of friends of the opposite sex, so I quickly moved past that and tried to get to know some of them.

I didn't like any of them. They all appeared to be falling all over our friend and competing for his attention. So now Kate and I have to try to stomach our way through an evening with a bunch of women in their 30's acting like teenagers.

The friend that invited us out that night has money. At the end of dinner, again, I'm an observer, I watched him go around to all his friends and throw in cash for their food. Not one of those "friends" of his declined to take his money. That really bothered me. Then he got to me and grabbed my check.

90

"How much was your dinner? Let me throw in twenty bucks."

"No. Absolutely not."

"What do you mean, no? Let me pitch in!"

"Pitch in? Are we on a date?"

"No."

"Alright then, I'm paying for my own dinner."

Which brings me to another red flag: If I don't like his friends...or if he doesn't like mine. I never went out with his "friends" again. In fact, the next time we did get together, I told him he needed to take inventory of his friends.

"I don't know them so I could be wrong, but not one of those girls turned you down when you started throwing your money around. Are they friends with you because of who you are or because of your money?"

It wasn't an easy conversation, but he respected me for being honest about what I observed that night. I didn't like what I saw. It's great when you're in a place where you can bless your friends. I love being able to do something nice financially for my friends who might not make as much money as I do, but it's another thing when they start hanging around *because* of your money. That's something only you can discern. But if you're doing more of the paying than they are, it's time to reevaluate. If your friends are always broke, eventually you will be too.

Be careful who you marry, people. Make good choices. When you get married, make really, really good choices.

~ Christopher Titus, from his standup special, Born with a Defect

I know what you're thinking; I have had a run of bad luck with men. Not exactly, you see, all these examples came from the same guy. I never saw him again after one of these exchanges. I got one text from him the day after our last dinner that I didn't respond to because that dinner ended with some awkward, inappropriate words and I didn't feel so much like talking to him anymore, and the next thing I know I was unfriended on Facebook. Maybe I wasn't compliant enough, who knows. I never asked. I will rarely go after any friend who can so quickly write me off...but I will block your phone number, and you will never hear from me again.

I wish this friendship had a different ending, but it is what it is. There were times when I had a lot of fun with him, and I do miss that side of him. I probably should have nipped whatever this was a couple of years ago, but it caught me off guard. I did the best I could at the time with whatever unclear signals he was throwing at me. Lesson learned.

The right guy is out there. I'm just not going to kiss a whole bunch of losers to get to him.

~ from the movie, Never Been Kissed

I used to plan months in advance for New Year's Eve, making sure that I had plans in place, so there was no chance of getting forgotten, overlooked or God forbid, pitied for having no plans. In 2014 Kate came over, and we played board games and danced in my living room to Elton John singing "I'm Still Standing" after the ball dropped. In 2015 we went to the Tempe Improv and back to her house for movies. In keeping with that pattern, I made sure to lock her down in advance for New Year's Eve, 2016.

As the weeks got closer to New Years, neither one of us was talking to the other about what to do that night.

She had just moved a few weeks before, so I thought maybe she was tired and not up for doing anything or perhaps she got another invite and didn't want to hurt my feelings. I decided to go forward with my own plans, and if she called me, we'd get together like we always do. If not, I was going to have the best New Year's Eve I've ever had all by myself.

New Year's Eve 2016 I met a friend at the gym followed by coffee at Starbucks. When I left Starbucks, I drove to my favorite Chinese place (I miss that place) and ordered an obscene amount of food to go. My plan: Chinese food, beer, and movies. If somebody called to invite me out, that's great. If not, I was set for the evening. While I do enjoy going out, I equally enjoy sitting at home watching movies. This was a win/win for me.

I did get one phone call that night. I was shocked and pleasantly surprised when my phone rang around 6 pm. Okay! Somebody wants to hang out!

"Hey, do you have plans tonight?"

"No, I don't. I'm just eating dinner and watching a movie."

"Oh." (She said with a sad tone in her voice) "I would invite you out, but I'm with my boyfriend and its couples only."

THEN WHY ARE YOU CALLING ME?! For those of you who are coupled and have single friends, stop doing this shit! I have nothing against couples only. However, I do have something against couples only and making it a huge deal to your single friends.

Saying you would invite me out if it weren't couples only is worse than if you didn't bring it up at all. Couples only aside, if I'm not whole enough to spend time with as a single woman, don't you dare call me after I'm in a relationship. When I do meet somebody, I don't want my

93

phone being suddenly blown up by people who never spent time with me as a single woman and are now asking for a double date. I promise you, the answer will be no.

It's not about holding a grudge, and this doesn't make me high maintenance. I'm not sitting around and letting anger take over because they are not meeting my unrealistic expectations. It's about raising the bar in ALL relationships. I don't like being a back burner friend; somebody you call when better plans fall through. I don't in any way mean to imply that I'm perfect. I've dropped the ball more than one time in my life. I have given grace to others who disappointed me and have been given mercy when I fell short.

As I said before, I'm very loyal and don't walk away from friendships easily, but I do watch behavior patterns. If I'm doing all the asking out, at some point, I'm going to stop until you ask me. I'm too old for one-sided friendships.

CHAPTER SIX

It's supposed to be hard. If it wasn't hard, everyone would do it. The hard is what makes it great.

~ from the movie, A League of Their Own

While I have an extroverted personality, I unwind like an introvert. I enjoy being with my friends about as much as I enjoy being home alone. With that said, there are days where it would be nice to have somebody to share a movie with, or go to the gym with, or fix the handle on my dresser when it just randomly pops off one morning out of the blue.

You are dependent on you and you alone. When a movie that you want to see hits the theatre, and you can't find a friend to see it with, it's party of one. When you know you should go to the gym, but you don't feel like it, it's *you* that has to motivate you to go. And when you open your dresser drawer in the morning while getting ready for work that you're already late for and the handle pops off, it's *you* that has to figure out which screwdriver to use to put said handle back on the dresser all the while reminding God this is not your job. Thanking Him, of course, that you're not an idiot and can fix it yourself, but anxiously awaiting the day when you can turn that job over to your husband.

Having a life that you enjoy fully does not mean you're free from bad days. What makes those bad days so lonely is feeling like you have nobody you can talk to. I'm the last single one in my family and most of my friends. It was easy before when I had single friends who could relate to my bad days.

It gets worse the older you get. The single friends you used to run with are suddenly all paired off and starting new lives, and you feel like you're in everybody's rear view mirror.

Sometimes being forgotten is okay. I don't like always being needed, but when the phone call frequency is non-existent and attempts to reach out appear to be falling on deaf ears, there is a part of me that wonders if anybody *really* needs me. It's hard being the friend who always gets phone calls for no reason to suddenly having nobody call because now there's a boyfriend and I'm not needed as much anymore.

Not all friends are like that all of the time, and of course, I know they love me, but it feels like my responsibilities as a friend have changed. It's like an unspoken demotion.

(Internal Dialogue) "See, you're not as cool as you think you are."

Because I don't do well with super needy friends, and now I'm finding myself in this place where I appear to be that super needy person, my instinct is to withdraw. The last thing I want to do is be the annoying, lonely, needy single friend.

So I stop everything. No texting. No phone calls. I stick to my routine. Eventually, somebody will realize they haven't talked to me in a while and call...., right? I could reach out, but if I send two or three texts over a couple of days and there is no response, I end up feeling pathetic. I would rather withdraw than allow myself to feel rejected or worse, end up annoying the other person.

Sometimes more than a week will go by and finally my phone rings. That's usually when my internal dialogue goes completely berserk.

Caller: "Hey, I just realized I haven't talked to you in forever!"

Me: (Oh, so you did notice) "Yes, it has been a while."

Caller: "How are you?"

Me: (as if you care) "I'm fine." (How is your stupid boyfriend?)

And then I proceed to verbally throw up on the unsuspecting caller about all the boring, non-life threatening events that have transpired in my incredibly boring life these past few days that feel more like years! (God help me am I high maintenance?)

Now my life is anything but boring, but in these moments of self-pity, it's hard to see it any other way. A bad attitude can really affect the way we view life around us.

For me, friendships are tested not in the best of times, but in the worst of times. You don't always get a second chance to be there for someone when they really need you. So when I say I will be there, I mean it.

~ Leah Remini, from her book Troublemaker

When a friend starts dating, that friendship usually changes in one way or another. As selfish as it sounds and it is selfish, it's hard taking a back seat to a new boyfriend when you've gotten used to being the go-to friend. As long as both friends make an effort and are honest with each other, I don't think it has to be as hard as some people make it. You also have to remember there are two sides to this. It's new territory for both friends. Some of my friendships have stayed intact and have even become stronger, and some of them are a constant battle.

THE DITCHER: One who will drop you hard when they get asked out.

Don't be a ditcher! If you get asked out for a night where you already have plans with a friend, tell him you have plans. What's the problem here? If a man wants to take you out, believe me, he will work around your schedule, and if he doesn't, you don't want him anyways. It's not about playing hard to get. It's about simply being a person who keeps your word. It shows your date that you have a life outside of him (which trust me is a good thing) and it shows the friend you already have plans with that they are important to you.

I completely understand that sometimes things come up and you have to reschedule. I'm talking about those who consistently break plans with you and only call when something with the boyfriend falls through. I also hate the phrase "I forgot." Even if you did forget, all it does is show me that I'm not important to you. It's always a lame excuse.

It all goes back to balance; time with your date, time with your friends and for me personally, time alone. If that relationship falls apart and you haven't invested any time in your friends, you're going to find yourself all alone.

If you're going to completely ignore my advice on being a ditcher, at least be honest about it. "Look, I have been waiting my entire life for this guy to ask me out (because in my mind people like this are overly dramatic as well) and I would really, really appreciate it if you would let me off the hook so I can go out with him." In this case, I don't have as much cause to be annoyed because at least they were honest with me.

I don't think ditchers have bad intentions. I was a ditcher in my twenties. I wouldn't think twice about ditching a friend for a guy who asked me out. I remember those years as being fully consumed with whatever guy I was interested in at the time, and my friends took a back seat to him. I allowed that new love interest to steal all my focus.

It's not that my friends were no longer important to me. Perhaps I got too comfortable in those friendships. I think it's very easy, especially the more longevity you have with some friendships, to take people for granted. Maybe the feeling of security you have with them makes it easier to put them on the back burner. Every relationship, no matter how much longevity you have, needs to be maintained. Be careful not to fall into the trap of complacency with your friends.

As I got older, balance began to play a more important role in my life. As much fun as it is spending time with somebody new or with an established relationship, I need to also have time with my friends and time alone to unwind.

We all have something to offer the world in some way, but by not being our authentic selves, we are robbing the world of something different, something special.

~ Leah Remini, from her Troublemaker book

The Snob: One who becomes completely unrecognizable after they start dating.

This is the worst kind, in my opinion. This person makes it clear that they are in a completely different league than you because they've started dating. They have a more condescending tone, and their body language shows a feeling of patronizing superiority.

I was once the third wheel at a dinner with this type. Thank God it was just the one time. It was my first time meeting her boyfriend. I am not the type to put on my "best behavior." That doesn't mean I'm unrestrained and obnoxious (I am aware of my audience), but I'm going to be myself and hope we find something in common.

We got along quite well. We had a lot in common, so there was no awkward silence in our conversation; we talked about movies and music and laughed a lot. If a good friend meets somebody and we get along, that's a win for me and my friend, right?

Not this friend. She sat there the entire time rolling her eyes and sipping her wine. I noticed it, but it wasn't the place to bring it up, so I shelved her bad attitude and went on with the evening like it wasn't happening. At one point in the middle of me talking, she held up her index finger to me, turned to her boyfriend and whispered something in his ear. When she was finished, she turned back to me and said, "Continue."

At this point in my life, she was one of my closest friends so you can imagine what was going through my mind. Who is this girl?!? We got a little loud at one point in our conversation when the boyfriend and I realized we were both huge Journey fans and in addition to her eye rolling she added an annoyed "Oh my god you guys, really??"

I don't hang out with snobs. I don't like snobs. I don't have time for snobs. All of a sudden, my close friend has transformed into a snob right in front of my eyes. I was caught entirely off guard...or was I?

Let's break this down a little. The red flags for this type of person can usually be detected before they morph into a snob. You can tell because they act one way when you're alone with them and completely different when other people are around.

When you're alone with them, they're vulnerable. You both feel free to laugh and cry and be yourself. But if any other person enters that circle all of a sudden the things about you they once thought were funny are now embarrassing to them. And they'll tell you too.

At a glance, I had nothing in common with this friend. I had other friends tell me they didn't see what we could possibly have to talk about. She was the wine and cheese type, and I was the beer and pretzel type. We were very different people, but we did have a lot of fun together and for a time had what I thought was a genuine friendship.

I did notice a change in her personality whenever other people came out with us. One night at dinner, with two other girlfriends, we were talking about relationships, and I made a joke (that I won't repeat). Usually, that joke gets a pretty good laugh, and it did from the other two girls. My friend, however:

"Stephanie, that's not funny."

"It was a joke. Lighten up."

"Many a truth is said in jest."

Confused by her pretentious choice of words, I responded with, "Why are you talking like that?"

It left me stunned. Where is my friend who laughed when I made a joke and was pretty funny herself? This girl sat up straighter and wasn't laughing at anything. I believe this type of behavior is rooted in insecurity. They may have let *you* see who they really are, but they don't dare show that side of themselves to anybody else.

The most important kind of freedom is to be what you really are. You trade in your reality for a role. You trade in your sense for an act. You give up your ability to feel, and in exchange, put on a mask. There can't be any large-scale revolution until there's a personal revolution, on an individual level. It's got to happen inside first.

~ Jim Morrison

It has to be a miserable existence, not being able to be yourself all the time. I'd rather be completely authentic and hated by many than put on a fake version of myself and be loved by everybody. What was extremely painful for me was the fact that she was visibly embarrassed to be with me. I battled that for months after the friendship ended in spite of many attempts to repair it.

It's okay if the friendship changes. Either you accept where it's landed, or you say goodbye and move on. As painful as some of these experiences have been, I'm grateful for them. It's made me more aware of who I want to be when a relationship finds me. I want to be as stable a friend when I'm in a relationship as I am single.

Phoebe: I have something for you. It's my little black book. Its got the numbers of all the guys I've dated.

Rachel: Phoebe, that's nice, but you know what, I think I'm okay. Why don't you give it to one of your other single girlfriends?

Phoebe: I would, but you're the last one.

~ FRIENDS, the TV show

My biggest fear of being the last single person among my group of friends is that I'll be forgotten. As friends start dating, the less frequent the incoming phone calls are. Friends who were hard to get together with before the boyfriend are now damn near impossible to get together with. It's hard not to take that personally.

(Internal Dialogue) "See, it's not that they didn't want to go out to dinner and a movie. They didn't want to do that with you."

The fear of being forgotten is a really tough thought to fight off. It's these types of fears that I feel I can't discuss with anybody. I'm afraid if I express them to my newly dating friends, then I might be perceived as being jealous. If I keep quiet and isolate myself, I might be seen as not being supportive.

What I try to focus on in cases like this are the friendships that haven't changed. It's so easy to become consumed with the one friend who vanishes instead of seeing the ones that are still standing right next to you. I did this for a good couple of months after one of my closest friendships came to an end. I'm so glad I didn't chase those friends away with the amazing pity party I was throwing for myself.

I was praying one day about how painful it was losing this friend of mine when the Holy Spirit gently reminded me that I'm focusing too much on what I lost instead of what I still have. Yes, that friend is gone. Yes, it was painful. But I am not alone. It almost happened overnight when these two friends started reaching out to me weekly to get together. And one of them was a newlywed! Her random texts, "I need to see you!" meant more to me than she will ever know. Just the other day she text me, "When can I see you? It's been years!" It had been a week. I love her.

There's also the group of friends who try to relate to me and act like they understand what I'm going through when they got married right out of high school and have no idea what it's like to watch everybody move on to new phases of life, and you feel like you've been left in the shallow end of the pool to entertain yourself.

Remember the trip to Vegas I took with my sister and brother-in-law? While the Vegas trip was business related, and I was with people I knew and loved, there were times where it was really hard. I was there with two other couples. It's so hard sometimes being single in those situations when you're the only one without a plus one, and it usually hits you out of nowhere. At times I felt awkward, I had a hard time feeling like I fit in and one night, in particular, I just wanted to be left alone. I didn't even really know why.

How do you explain to your sister that you're feeling weird and you want to be alone, but you don't know why and you swear you're not mad about anything?? My sister ended up knocking on my hotel door for about five minutes before I finally let her in. "Stephanie! What's wrong? We love you!" I can laugh about that now. My sister does not let anything go. You're not allowed to have a moment. She will force her company on you until you feel better or you have convinced her you're okay...and I love her for that.

These "moments" are so random. I don't get that way in every scenario where I'm the only single one. I spent my 39th birthday with two different couples on back to back nights and didn't feel weird at all. I had so much fun that birthday being with friends and didn't feel like the third wheel for even a second. However, if I'm around both my married sisters at the same time, that's harder for me. Maybe it's because I'm the oldest and still single while they're both 14 years deep into their marriages. I don't know. It's a hard thing to dissect.

The thing to remember in these moments is that they're just feelings and feelings are fickle. Go back to what you know is true about yourself and talk back to the voices that tell you that you don't belong...or whatever the heck they're saying to you in those moments.

Do you know what I miss most? I miss girl talk! That doesn't mean I still don't have girl talk among my girlfriends who are paired off. I'm talking about the girl talk that goes on between two single girlfriends. It's totally different when it's between a single friend and the "in a relationship" friend.

When you're both single, you're both engaged in each other's ridiculous stories of chance encounters with cute boys that usually don't go anywhere, but it's still so much fun to talk about. It usually goes something like this:

Single friend #1: "So I'm at church, minding my own business when this too-good-looking-to-be-talking-to-me guy, walked over and said Hello, I don't believe we've met. What's your name?"

Single friend #2: "No way! Tell me everything! What did you say back?"

THIS is fun girl talk! Two girlfriends acting completely ridiculous about some guy they will most likely never see again.

When one of these single ladies gets a boyfriend, the same statement has a very different response.

In a relationship friend: "Look, don't read into it. Pray about it. Just take it slow and be yourself."

Did I miss something here? It's not like I got psychotic and said in a dramatic tone, "I found the one." I miss the old girl talk. In this scenario, I feel like I'm being talked at by a mother figure. I don't think they believe they're better than me, but there does appear to be an unofficial change in rank that seems to have taken place. There's a boyfriend now. They're smarter, wiser and have tons of unwanted advice to give at inappropriate times.

Get in a good mood! How hard is it to just decide to be in a good mood and then be in a good mood?

~ Lloyd Dobler, from the movie, Say Anything

Easier said than done, right? Wrong. It's okay to have a bad moment as long as that moment doesn't turn into days and weeks and before you know it you've invited several of your friends to your pity party, and now nobody wants to spend time with you. If you're so focused on the negative, you're going to miss the good that's happening all around you. And during these moments you have to be intentional in looking for it.

In the fall of 2017, I threw myself a pity party that lasted a couple of months. All of my friends had moved into relationships, and I felt very alone for the first time in a long time. I was shopping alone, going to a new church alone, going out to eat alone and going to movies alone.

I remember one incident where I was at my kitchen table, working on this chapter (so I was already feeling all kinds of emotional) when I got a text from a friend who said: "I met somebody and it was all God!" I silenced my phone and yelled...at my phone, "Really?   You said the last three were "all God" too! Are you sure this one wasn't "all EHarmony?!"

I was at work one day after months of feeling sorry for myself. No amount of classic rock coming through my headphones was drowning out the internal dialogue running through my brain.

(Internal Dialogue) "You see?   They've already forgotten about you. Why doesn't anybody want to be with you? Clearly, there's something wrong with you that even you can't see. It's just you now. Get used to being alone."

And then it happened; a song I've heard over and over again hundreds of times, but this time it was different.

* *Wait on me girl*

Cry in the night if it helps

But more than ever, I simply love you more than I love life itself

* I Guess That's Why They Call It The Blues Music by Elton John and Davey Johnstone; Lyrics by Bernie Taupin; Universal Music Publishing Group

My eyes immediately welled up with tears. At that moment, it wasn't my man Elton John singing (I adore him) it was God speaking to me. A weight began to lift off of me at that moment. It's as if Jesus was saying, please wait on me. Cry it out if you need to, but in the meantime, don't forget how much *I* love you.

On my 40th birthday, I ended up getting these lyrics tattooed on my shoulder blade. Tattoo #4! I still don't care about wedding photos! =)

There were several other songs in that same week that stuck out for me in new ways. I know this can be a debatable topic between some Christians, but it helped pull me out of a funk. God created each and every one of us, so He knows us better than anybody else ever could. Why wouldn't He choose to sometimes encourage me through something I love so much like music?

What music did God speak to me through? I'm glad you asked. I was in such a funk that God must have known I needed more than one message from him.

"Truly, Madly, Deeply" performed by Savage Garden:

** *Oh, can you see it, baby?*

You don't have to close your eyes. 'Cause it's standing right before you

All that you need will surely come

** Words and Music by Daniel Jones and Darren Hayes; Producer Charles Fisher; Sony/ATV Music Publishing LLC

During this song, I felt like God was telling me that He is standing right there with me and that He has a plan for me that will come to pass if I stay focused on Him. *"For I know the plans I have for you," says the Lord "They are plans for good and not for disaster, to give you a future and a hope." Jeremiah 29:11*

"Hold My Hand" performed by Hootie and the Blowfish:

*** *I've got a hand for you*

I wanna run with you

Won't you let me run with you? Hold my hand

*** Words and Music by Darius Carlos Rucker, Everett Dean Felber, Mark William Bryan, and James George Sonefeld; Sony/ATV Music Publishing LLC

This song made me cry because I felt like God was telling me that while I am busy feeling sorry for myself, He desires to spend time with me. *"Draw close to God, and He will draw close to you."* ~ *James 4:8* That is true for every single person on the planet. God desires to spend time with you.

"The One" performed by Backstreet Boys....I was in a 90's mood this week.

**** *I'll be the one who will make all your sorrows undone*

I'll be the light when you feel like there's nowhere to run

I'll be the one

**** Words and Music by Max Martin and Brian T. Littrell; Arranged by Dan Coates; copyright Kobalt Music Publishing Ltd

This song reminded me that God wants to be the one I turn to. He wants to be the one that I run to when I feel overwhelmed or have a bad day. When I feel like I'm all alone, He will be the one who is always there. Thank you, Backstreet Boys! *"Do not be afraid or discouraged, for the Lord is the one who goes before you. He will be with you; he will neither fail you nor forsake you."* *Deuteronomy 31:8*

Since I'm on a roll with sharing music, I would like to make an honorable mention to Metallica's, "Nothing Else Matters." This song without fail will magically appear on the radio just when I need it. It showed up during my break up in 2009. It popped up again when I was in the throes of my anxiety attacks. And sometimes it shows up when I need to bring my focus back to God.

I know what some of you are thinking. How does a Metallica song bring your focus back around to God? Well, it's all in how you hear the words. Did you and your friends ever have a song in high school? You know, where a song would come on the radio, and you would both shout, "It's our song!" I feel that way about this song with God. When it comes on the radio, I smile and say to God, "It's our song."

At the end of the day, no matter how blue you may feel or how crappy your life may appear to be in the moment, there is good in your life. And when it's just you, you're going to have to be intentional in looking for it. For me, music has played a huge part in bringing my focus back off of my problems and onto more important things. Spinning emotionally out of control and getting too into your head is so easy to do and good news, it's normal. Welcome to the human race. However, staying in that space should never be an option. Something as simple as watching one of my favorite movies or reading a new book can sometimes help pull me out of that funk.

I believe there is something that God wants me to do during this time of being single that I couldn't do if I were in a relationship. I think this book is one of those things. I couldn't have written this book if I was in a relationship. Well, technically I could, but I'm not sure it would have been as impactful if I was in a relationship. All it takes is one date to completely forget what it feels like to be single. I believe writing this book while I am in the throes of singleness is going to be far more impactful....at least I hope it is.

So what if I finish this book and I still haven't met somebody? Then I will need to figure out what the next thing is or at the very least, continue to enjoy my life doing the things I love.

CHAPTER SEVEN

*This was Girl World, and in Girl World, all the fighting had
to be sneaky.*

~ Mean Girls, the movie

Why do so many single women who can't seem to get their act together think they have the answers for everybody else's singleness?

"She's so picky she'll never find somebody to marry."

"He's so shy. It's probably why he's still single."

Let me tell you why this bothers me so much. I don't ever want to judge somebody else's "singleness" because I don't want them saying the same stupid things about me. It would really hurt me if I found out somebody was using a weakness of mine as their reason for why I'm still single. These girls are not observant; they're judgmental.

I've noticed a growing trend among some single women in churches. It's a particular group of women who run around silently calling dibs on every available, good looking man in the church. They travel in packs, I believe, because of the old saying *keep your friends close and your enemies closer.* They're all fighting with each other for the attention of the same group of men who in most cases don't even know they're alive. It's hilarious.

These women say things like, "He's always looking at me," and sometimes even say, "God told me he's my husband." Don't misunderstand me. I believe God does talk to everybody who will listen, but that is not what I am talking about in these cases.

Simply saying "God told me" doesn't make it true. I think this phrase gets thrown around too loosely and we should be more careful with how we use it. Plus, we don't need to tell everybody everything God says to us if only for the reason that sometimes we are wrong. I've been wrong more than once so I'm speaking out of experience as well.

These women position themselves to be right in front of these guys every chance they get and have never spoken one single word to them.

Because of this, you can't tell these girls about anything exciting thing that happens in your life. As soon as you do, they'll find a way to take it away from you. And it doesn't have to be a big romantic moment either. They'll steal something as simple as a kind gesture from the opposite sex. I call them Moment Stealers.

Moment Stealer Example #1: A guy at church gave me a Starbucks gift card on Valentine's Day. He had absolutely no agenda and in fact, gave a gift card to several single women at church just to bless them on what can be a hard day for some. It was a very sweet and thoughtful thing to do until a moment stealer said, "Don't read into it. I heard he likes me."

Moment Stealer Example #2: There's another guy at church who has been paying attention to me for years. From what I hear, he's paid attention to several different women. The difference is I've actually been out with him. The second I bring him up with other women in the church, it's the same line, "Oh, he does that to me all the time. It's not you. That dude hits on everybody."

I mean, really ladies? Even if it is true, why are we so quick to take these moments away from each other? For some women, these moments, wanted or unwanted, are few and far between, and even if they are unwanted, it still feels good to know somebody at the very least sees you. And what do you do? You steal their moment.

(Internal Dialogue) "See? It couldn't have possibly been you. He's not interested in you. He's interested in everybody which means you're nobody special. You're just somebody."

Moment Stealer Example #3: I am friends (literally, just friends) with an eligible guy in church and I use the word "eligible" based on a large number of women who claimed he was "the one." I had a family tragedy summer of 2016 and by family tragedy, I mean my cat peed all over my bedroom carpet and then died. As a single woman, dealing with something as emotional as this is really hard. My cat died, and now I have to figure out how to clean my carpet, which I've never done on my own before. It's moments like these where a husband would come in handy.

I rented a carpet cleaner from a local store down the street. Not that I needed him to, but the employee never offered to take it out to my car for me. Now I'm dragging this heavy carpet cleaner across the parking lot and trying to cram it into my Corolla (I may or may not have said a few colorful words while doing this) and I'm crying. He didn't have to help me but the fact that he didn't offer to help just added to my already crappy day. It reminded me that I was all alone in this.

I had no idea how to work this stupid carpet cleaner and felt I was in no way fit to figure it out. Not only that, even if I did figure it out, my bed was far too heavy for me to move even an inch all by myself. I stood in the middle of my bedroom and cried. "God, I need help."

It was 11 am on a Friday. The only one I could think of that might be available was my self-employed friend from church. So I called him and told him my predicament. He didn't sound inconvenienced even a little. In fact, he interrupted my plea for help and said: "I'll be there in ten minutes."

This guy not only took time out of his day to move my bed four different times so all the carpet could get cleaned, but he also cleaned it for me. That's a good friend. As a single woman I love and appreciate the male friends in my life because there are just some things I am not able to do myself and when they show up, it feels like God is taking care of me.

Naturally, I gave him a shout out on Facebook for being such a selfless friend. That Sunday, the single women came out of the four corners of that church to grill me on my relationship with him, and even after I assured them, he was just a friend.

"Be careful. I hear he flirts with everybody."

"I hear he asks out a lot of girls."

"He flirts with me all the time."

One Facebook post, about one friend, helping out another, and all the single women go berserk! This wasn't even what I consider "a moment," but that was enough to send some women over to me to make sure there was nothing romantic going on between us.

So what happens when a single friend enters a relationship, or God forbid gets married? That turns the judgmental women and moment stealers into straight up ugly women. It's embarrassing.

"I feel sorry for her. Have you seen them together? He clearly doesn't want to be with her." "Have you seen their baby? He's cute, but no thanks to her."

You're not fooling anybody, ladies. This screams jealousy for no reason other than you weren't the one who was picked. This behavior is unacceptable, unbecoming, and unattractive. Stop running around, calling dibs on every available man you see. It doesn't work like that. I don't understand why you would *want* it to.

Do you want a relationship that is built on you manipulating your way into that person's life? Or do you want a relationship that started with a man who saw you and said to himself, "That's the one! I HAVE to get to know her!" And he wasn't distracted by anybody else. His eyes were only on you. The choice is yours.

It can be hard waiting for somebody you are interested in to pursue you, but it will prevent the inevitable heartbreak that comes with manufacturing a relationship that was never meant to be.

I won't compete with anybody. If a man shows interest in me and someone else, where some women might turn up the heat and find new ways to keep his attention, I'm going to bounce. I will not share, and I will not *be* shared. I deserve, we all deserve, somebody who has eyes only for you. Be friendly. Treat him like you would anybody else in your life and if he asks out somebody else; good. Now you know he wasn't for you.

We need to do better, ladies. Not just with how we want to be treated, but with how we treat others. Instead of comparing and competing with your so-called friends, share in their excitement. Let them have the win. I promise it won't kill you.

When somebody endures a breakup, or a potential relationship doesn't work out, people love to throw around the phrase "it's his loss." Here's what I think; if he wasn't the one for you, then you weren't the one for him either. That means both people win.

On more than one occasion, my male friendships have come into question. This aggravates me on several different levels. One is the gossip factor. A group of girls get together and decide based on nothing that one of my male friends "likes me." I find this out from a third party and tell them it's simply not true. We are just friends. Except now, the words those girls have said are roaming around in my head, and suddenly I'm uncomfortable around that person who I once considered only a friend. It almost ruined a couple of friendships of mine.

My intentions seem to come into question even more as the only single one left in the group. I have one guy friend I am very close to. He dates a lot more than I do so every couple of months or so, whenever he has a girlfriend, the friendship changes, as it should since it is a male/female friendship. It's different with men. If one of my girlfriends gets a boyfriend, we can still take off for the weekend together and have dinner and go to movies. But if my male friend gets a girlfriend, I back off out of respect for the girlfriend.

On more than one occasion this friendship has been "called out" which I find silly because I've been nothing but honest about it from the beginning. What's frustrating about this is that I sit and listen to the "my boyfriend bought me this" and "my boyfriend bought me that" and "he's so awesome because he took me to this restaurant" but I make mention of one selfless thing this male friend does for me, and I get "Stephanie, do you have feelings for him?"

Let me just say this. I'm sharing so I can feel like I'm a part of the conversation. If the discussion is always "relationship," and I'm not in one, I'm going to try to find a way to contribute to the conversation. I want to play too! And if I'm sharing in the wonderful things that your boyfriend is doing for you, please share in the wonderful things that are happening to me too and don't assume there are "feelings" behind it.

Now, just for kicks, let's speak to the other side of this. If you are the single friend and you've had your heart broken, don't piss on your friends' happy relationship. Just be happy for them and keep your painful past to yourself in these circumstances. Treat them how you would want to be treated if it was you who was in the relationship talking to a single friend. Sometimes it takes practice but trust me; it feels better to be happy for somebody rather than projecting your bad past relationship issues on them.

With all that said, I quit sharing my moments. I believe it's much simpler this way. I've had many amazing moments with some really nice men that were just that...moments. I've had lots of long eye contact, nice conversations, and progressing friendships that had promise but didn't end in a date. I never found out whether or not there were feelings there at one point, but I'm okay with that. It shouldn't matter. If they were interested in pursuing me, they would have continued. I look at those "moments" as a friendly reminder from God; He hasn't forgotten about me.

CHAPTER EIGHT

Life moves pretty fast. If you don't stop and look around once in a while, you could miss it.

~ from the movie, Ferris Bueller's Day Off

If I look over my life, I guess I've always been directing in one way or another. My sisters and I used to make these goofy home movies when we were kids with my Uncle Fred's camcorder (it was the 90s). We would write skits with quick costume changes so we didn't leave the camera on pause too long or it would stop and mess up the tape.

In one skit, I wanted my sister Joanna to play mom AND daughter. I had a song by Prince on a cassette tape that I held up to the camcorder microphone and my sister (playing the daughter) was dancing and singing to the song *The Most Beautiful Girl In The World* when "mom" knocks on the door (my sister Melinda knocked). I hit pause, and Joanna does a quick costume change into the part of "mom," I hit record and now Joanna, as the mom, says her lines.

But, the knock at the door had to happen on a specific beat of the song. I was very particular, even at age 13, about things like that. I remember being at a wedding when I was in high school and thinking to myself, man, if the bride walked in on this beat of that song instead of that beat it would have been a way more dramatic entrance. I guess you could call that directing.

By January 2016, I now had two full years in the media department at church. I had also landed a job as a contractor for a local television studio that had video shoots once a month. One of the graphics volunteers at church asked me if I was interested in coming into the studio where she worked as a floor director and run camera. I said as long as it didn't interfere with church or work I would love to.

One week later, she called and said, "So, they don't want you to run a camera. They want you to direct."

And just like that, I'm directing in an actual television studio! I had so much vacation time at my full-time job, and they've always been supportive of my side career so as long as my schedule at work was clear, I was able to direct at the studio. I did it about twelve times total in a year and a half period. It was quite an experience.

While all that was exciting, I felt like all the things I was doing to fully enjoy my life as a single woman had suddenly taken a backseat to this media career. Not to say that the time I spent in the Media department wasn't worth it. I wouldn't have a media resume if it weren't for all the time I invested in learning and developing those skills, but now it was time to bring things into balance.

Most of my friends during this time were very understanding. I wrote earlier about being a person who keeps her word, and I do believe in that firmly, but I rescheduled many sushi nights because I had a last minute call from the church that required me to cancel plans with friends.

I made it clear to my friends that at this particular time in my life, media at church was my priority. I would never cancel plans with one friend for better plans with another, but if church called, I dropped everything and ran. I treated it like a job; a job that was building me a media resume.

I always loved the idea of traveling but added it to my list of things to do after I'm married. Here I am, single, I have this great job with a ton of vacation time, and I am not traveling; mostly because I didn't have anybody to go with. Let's face it, being married doesn't mean you'll always have somebody to do stuff with either but at least there's somebody there. It's literally just me right now.

I started thinking about all the friends and family I have across this great country. Why not pick a few places I've never been before where I have friends or family and get my traveling in that way? I wouldn't have to worry about getting a rental car or a hotel. I could visit a new state and see friends and family.

March 2016, Dallas, Texas

I had driven through Texas before but to me, driving through a state doesn't count as actually having been to that state. Seeing the spot where Kennedy was shot was a place I had always wanted to visit and I just so happen to have a friend who lives in Dallas. We took the train to Dealey Plaza and took the Book Depository tour. He took me to his favorite club that had amazing live music and to his favorite bar that had great food! It was so much fun!

I found myself back in Dallas two weeks later because this same friend ended up having knee surgery and didn't have any family or friends in town who could help him out that week after his surgery. Two trips to Texas in one month! My plan appeared to be working. I traveled to a new state where I had never been before to visit a friend and did some site seeing. Where else could I go?

May 2016, Elk River, Minnesota

Now Minnesota is a state I've obviously been to before (I was born and raised there), but the reason for the trip is what stood out for me. Tom Barnard is a Minnesota radio legend. I've been listening to him for 20+ years on the KQ Morning Show, a very popular morning show on a classic rock station. He also has a podcast, The Tom Barnard Show that he does with his wife and their son and daughter. At a silent auction for a fundraiser for her my niece's school, my sister won an in-studio experience for two on his podcast. I was so excited I could hardly talk!

I listen to this guy via podcast five days a week and now, all of a sudden, I'm sitting in between him and Michele Tafoya from NBC's Sunday Night Football. Ian Leonard, who is a meteorologist from the local FOX news channel, popped in for hour two along with Rick Bronson from Rick Bronson's House of Comedy.

Talk about a strange and exciting experience! I remember when Tom's wife, Kathryn came out to welcome my sister and I and I gave an enthusiastic "HI!" and this voice in my head said, "Take it down a notch. You might feel like you know them, but they do not know you." HA! I was so consumed with nerves I'm convinced I looked crazed for the first hour of the show.

I've met a lot of fun celebrities over the years, but I was so excited to meet Tom. Every single person in that room was so much fun and easy to talk to. At one point he asked me where I was from and when I said Phoenix he said, "Oh! Phoenix! What a hot shot!" I smiled and said to myself, "He's picking on me! This is great!"

It's a strange feeling when you're suddenly in a small room looking at and talking with the same people you have been listening to for years. It was so much fun.

I found myself back in Minnesota that August because God forbid I miss one year of the Minnesota State Fair. I was also in Minnesota in December of 2015 for Christmas (I rarely go back for Christmas). While I go to Minnesota every summer, the three trips I took in less than a year were an unexpected and pleasant surprise.

October 2016, Portland, Oregon

I flew to Portland, Oregon, to visit my childhood friend Sarah and her wife, Janell. I've known Sarah for well over 30 years but had limited interaction with Janell only because we didn't live anywhere near each other. It was an excellent opportunity for us to get to know each other.

121

My first night there, we went to a brewery for dinner. We talked about this book that I had not yet begun to start writing and other things, but the discussion was heavy on relationships. And then Janell said something that changed the way I looked at marriage from that day forward:

In our wedding vows, we promised that we would never have to celebrate or fight anything alone, ever again.

That was the beginning of me digging deeper into what I wanted in a marriage. I never looked at it the same since that day. I remember thinking to myself, I could have an average marriage and be pretty happy, or I could start digging deeper and work toward an extraordinary marriage.

Portland was my most memorable trip of 2016 in that while I was there I discovered something that was missing in my life. In Oregon, I felt peace. I was still. I was quiet. The weather was overcast and in the 50s. I flew in on a Wednesday night and had their house to myself that Thursday and Friday while they were at work. I listened to Joyce Myer podcasts and did devotionals. The front door was open with a cool breeze coming in. I snuggled on their sofa, surrounded by their kitties reading a book I had bought the night before. I read for hours. I prayed. It was the first time in a long time when I felt complete rest.

That weekend, the three of us drove to the ocean in Astoria. I ran up and down the beach with the ocean at my feet. I did a few really bad cartwheels on the sand just because I could. We drove to Roloff Farms and even got to meet some of the Roloff family and buy some of their amazing pumpkin salsa.

I felt the most alive I've felt in a long time. I knew then I had to make some changes at home if I wanted that feeling to last. I was completely out of balance. My intentions were good in training to become a director, but I was overworked, tired, and unhappy. If the thing you love doing the most is no longer fun, there's a problem. It was also keeping me completely distracted from what it is God wanted me to do; write this book.

The changes I knew I had to make scared the crap out of me. I had spent the last three years in Media at my church. Two of those years I spent directing. I felt like I was finally doing something that I was born to do, but it was also consuming all my free time. Portland was the first time in a long time I felt rest. I had no rest in my life.

I heard Joyce Meyer once say, *"If you don't like your schedule, change it. God didn't call you to be busy."* It sounds so easy. Was it really that easy? I was so busy with a full-time job, volunteering on Wednesdays and weekends, and trying to find time to maintain friendships somewhere in there. But she was right. I had to put aside what other people expected of me and ask God what He wanted me to do. The more I prayed about it, the more I felt it was time to cut back from my volunteering in media.

I think this is a real test of faith. Being able to let go of something you love and follow where you believe God is leading you even though what you want is so close you can almost touch it, shows God that above all, you're following Him. It's not something I just decided to do. It's something I prayed about for a couple of months and taking a step back, while scary, gave me peace.

It's not hard to follow God. You don't have to be a rocket scientist or genius to follow the Holy Spirit. You just have to follow the presence or absence of peace.

~ Joseph Prince, from his book, Live the Let-Go Life

This isn't the first time I've come close to something that I had waited a long time for, and I felt God saying, "I know you really want this, but I'm asking you to lay it down. There's something else I need you to do."

I had an opportunity to be an extra in a movie that was being shot in Arizona during the summer of 2015. A friend of mine at the time had recently started doing some acting. She told me they were looking for extras and she asked if I wanted to go with. I quickly said, yes.

It wasn't the opportunity to be an extra in a movie that excited me. I couldn't have cared less about that. I was excited at the possibility of making connections with the filmmakers in hopes of getting my foot in the door and expanding my media career beyond my church doors. A few days before the Saturday shoot, as I was telling my friend Pastor Cynthia how excited I was, I got a text from the video director at my church.

"I know you asked for Saturday off, but something came up, and the church needs me in another building shooting B-roll. Is there any way you can direct on Saturday?"

My heart sunk, and my eyes immediately welled up with tears. I had waited for this opportunity for years. It was right in front of me. I thought for sure this was it and now I'm faced with a choice. I always said that no matter what other media jobs came up, church would always be my number one. If I meant that, I knew what I had to do.

Even though my heart hurt at the loss of an opportunity, I took a deep breath and responded with, "Of course. I'll be there."

My actor friend didn't take the news well. I should have seen this as the beginning of the end of our friendship. I was so upset about having to cancel, but I believe I made the right decision. Her response had a tone that indicated I was a complete moron for the decision I made.

"Are you serious Stephanie? They're not even paying you." Her gig wasn't a paid gig either, so I'm not sure what point she was trying to make with that other than making sure I knew I was making a terrible decision.

It was never about the money. It still isn't. I decided when all this started that I would take any and all other media opportunities that came my way as long as it didn't interfere with media at church. I never took a directing job at the television studio if it interfered with church. The church job came first. I felt at the time and still do that I wouldn't be able to learn as much if I was loosely committed to several different projects. But if I fully committed to one (church) and took other jobs as they came along, then there was some stability in my training.

I heard a pastor once say that following Jesus sometimes means being misunderstood. I hate being misunderstood.

My friend, being a Christian herself, should have understood why I chose to back out of that movie. But she didn't and was pretty pissed off at me for some time. She even told me that I embarrassed her, which is ridiculous. There were hundreds of extras for that shoot. I'm positive they didn't miss me.

Since it was now November, and under no circumstances would I ever step back during the Christmas production, I decided January of 2017, I would take off entirely. In February I would go back for two weekends and two Wednesdays a month; leaving me with two weekends a month where I didn't have to work in media ultimately ending in REST for me. Rest for my body, rest for my mind and room for relationships to strengthen and grow once again.

I'm glad I stayed through the Christmas 2016 season because I ended up directing ALL 16 Christmas Productions that year. To be able to say I have directed 16 Broadway-style productions on my media resume is pretty cool for somebody who is just getting started.

I also knew I had a book to write; this book. I had talked about writing it, journaled for years, and I was fully aware that it would never get written if I was knee deep in volunteer work at church and a full-time job. I felt like the time had come to put this book together.

January 2017, I officially started writing this book. I also continued traveling.

In April 2017, I flew to Tulsa, Oklahoma, and spent some time with my sisters. My Minnesota sister drove with her husband and daughter and met me there.

In May 2017, my sister Melinda and I flew to Las Vegas. One night we went and saw The Beatles Cirque show LOVE. Being huge Beatles fans, we both cried our eyes out. We also cleaned out the merchandise store!

Another night we went and saw my other favorite band, Journey. When we got to the venue, we went to the merchandise table first so we wouldn't have to battle the lines after the show. Jonathan Cain (my favorite...I told you I had a thing for men who played the piano) had just released a solo album that was for sale at their merchandise table.

Of course, I purchased the CD and told the girl behind the table how cool it was that he was selling it at the show. She said, "He will be signing copies after the show if you want to come back." I swear there was a minute-long pause where I just stared at her. I couldn't believe that he was actually going to be signing his CD after the show. I was going to get to shake hands with Jonathan Cain!!! (I'm such a nerd)

In June 2017, I drove to San Diego with a couple of girlfriends for the weekend. We spent time at the ocean on Coronado Island with a cooler full of beer and bags of Cheetos. I sat on my chair and read a book, took a short nap and people watched. I love people watching!! Later that night, we went to a piano bar for dinner and live music.

That same summer I also got some very expensive seats and took my best friend to see New Kids on the Block, Boyz II Men, and Paula Abdul. You only live once, right? It was totally worth it! Not only were the seats amazing but these guys, NKOTB, scattered themselves all across the arena and started climbing up into the seats, shaking hands and taking pictures with fans. I've never seen anything like it before in my life. Jonathan Knight and Donnie Wahlberg both climbed into our section. I gained a whole new respect for those boys that night. They really love their fans!

I also bought an original painting by Val Kilmer, which got me a meet and greet with him at the very first annual Doc Holiday's event in Tombstone, Arizona. That was such a tough decision for me to make I called my dad. What I love about my dad is that if he thinks it's a dumb idea, he won't hesitate to tell me. I told him how much the painting was and asked if he thought it was a dumb idea. My dad, being a Tombstone fan himself, said, "I don't know Steph. It sounds pretty cool to me. I'd pull the trigger on that if I were you." So I did. And I got to shake hands and have a chat with Mr. Val Kilmer.

As summer came to a close, I began to feel more and more that my taking a step back from media was heading more towards a step-down. I had been at this church for fifteen years; the last four have been life changing in regards to my media career.

I remember two years earlier during one of our summer musicals I was walking in the first balcony before the lights were even on. I remember saying to myself; I can't believe I attend this church. And I get to direct services. I can't believe they gave me keys to this place. I feel so lucky to be a part of all of this.

At that moment, I felt God say to me, "You know, I might ask you to leave someday." I felt fearful for just a second, and then I simply nodded my head and said, "We will cross that bridge when we come to it."

And now I found myself at that bridge with that all too familiar voice whispering, "I know you really want this, but I'm asking you to lay it down. There's something else I need you to do."

I did what I set out to do the beginning of 2017. That February through September, I dug my heels in about only working two weekends and two Wednesdays. Sometimes things came up, and I ended up working more than planned, but for the most part, I stuck to those rules.

On September 20th, 2017, I walked out of the control room for the last time. I walked down the side stairs, across the main stage, through the lobby and out the door to my car. I cried the whole way home.

CHAPTER NINE

What is it like to be married to me?

~ Noelle Larson, Gateway Church, Scottsdale

It was 6 am on a Saturday. I had just got home from the gym. I still had 90's music playing loudly on my phone. I found myself in the kitchen, dancing, and singing while making breakfast. Then it hit me. What if he was here right now?

What if in this moment of scrambling eggs and dancing, I was married. Would he be sleeping? Would he yell from the other room to turn the music down? (I sure hope not) Would he lie in bed and think to himself how lucky he was to have such an awesome, free-spirited wife who danced and sang while making breakfast as if nobody was watching her? Would he think to himself, that's what you get for marrying a woman who doesn't always act her age?

I started to look around my apartment. What routine did I currently have that may or may not irritate this imaginary husband of mine? I opened up my refrigerator. Everything is in its place, and by everything I mean the few things I actually have in my fridge. I grocery shop twice a week and I never buy more than I can eat in a five day period.

Eggs and deli sliced chicken on the bottom shelf. Cheese and protein bars are on the second shelf and my Brita water pitcher on the top shelf. The door of my refrigerator holds greek yogurt, protein shakes, coffee, and coffee creamer and in my pantry one five pound bag of rice, a bag of cashews and a lot of dusty cookbooks. My freezer is even sadder ...one bag of frozen mango and an ice pack.

I know single women who have a full freezer, fridge, and pantry like they have a family of 5 at home. I have just never shopped like that. It creates too much room for spoiled food. What if he shops like he has a family of five? What if he comes over and starts moving all my stuff around? Would that annoy me?

I'm not trying to sound all *Sleeping with the Enemy* as if all my canned peas, if I had canned peas, have to be facing the same way or I'll go berserk, and these are not typically things that bother me, but I did think about it and that in turn got me to think about other things.

My morning routine during an average work week is pretty much the same. I'm not including days where I might go to a movie or have dinner with a friend. It's an average weekday of mine with no other plans.

My alarm goes off between 4:15 am and 4:45 am depending on what is going on at work that week. I rarely hit snooze because I'm one of those annoying morning people who wakes up and I'm ready to start the day. I can also attribute that to getting between 7 and 9 hours of sleep every night. I'm usually pretty well rested in the morning.

I get out of bed and pull the covers up, so my cats don't get their fur all over my sheets.

(Internal Dialogue) "What if he hates animals?" HA! I can't even say that with a straight face. I would never in a million years date a guy who hated animals. That's a deal breaker for me. "What if he's not a morning person? What if he stays up late? What if he leaves the bed a mess every morning and my cats run amuck on my sheets?"

I grab my cell phone charger and whatever book I'm currently reading and walk into the living room and put them in my work bag. It's always on the floor at the end of my sofa. There is no real reason for that. That's just where I put it.

(Internal Dialogue) "Does that make me a slob for leaving my work bag out like that? I hope he doesn't think I'm a slob."

Then I walk into the kitchen and take two multivitamins. My vitamins are sitting out on the kitchen counter next to my rice cooker, an unused spice rack and a statue of W.C. Fields that's less than two feet tall.

(Internal Dialogue) "What if he wants me to put my vitamins in the pantry? What if he is a super neat freak and can't have things out on the counter? It wouldn't kill me to put my vitamins in the pantry, but I'm not moving W.C. Fields! If he wants it moved he can build me a super awesome display shelf for him...I probably shouldn't assume he can build things but wouldn't that be handy?"

I head over to the bathroom, set my cell phone on the counter, and start the shower. My pajamas get tossed on the floor, and my unmentionables (why can't I just say underwear? I haven't been remotely reserved in my writing so far) get tossed in the hallway and will stay there until I get home from work.

(Internal Dialogue) "It's like I can already hear him asking me why are your underwear always on the hall floor?

After my shower and I mean right after I'm out of the shower, I fire up the Podcast app on my phone, and it pretty much stays on for the next ten to eleven hours. I'm a podcast nerd. I currently subscribe to fifteen podcasts. Two of them have gone dark, but I won't delete them just in case they decide to come back.

(Internal Dialogue) "I hope I can still listen to podcasts while I get ready for work."

By the time I'm dressed, my hair is done, and what little makeup I do wear has been applied to my eyes, my bathroom looks like this. The bathmat has been neatly placed back on the tub, my hairdryer is on top of the toilet because that's just where I put it, and I have one small makeup bag that may or may not be on the counter. My pajamas are on the bathroom floor in a ball...usually, a kitty sleeping on top of them by now.

I pick up said kitty from my pajamas and close the bathroom door. I have the world's most curious cats, and they get into everything. For that reason, the bathroom door is always closed.

(Internal Dialogue) "What if he always forgets to close that door? I've had friends over who leave the toilet seat up AND leave the bathroom door open. I can already imagine my cats knocking things off the counter."

With my cell phone in my back pocket (podcasts playing) I stop in the hallway, not to pick up my clothes off the floor, but to adjust the thermostat because, as I write this, its summer in Arizona and the at-home temp is different than the not-at-home temp which is also different from the while-I'm-sleeping temp.

(Internal Dialogue) "Is he going to be one of those weird guys who loves the heat, or is he going to be a bank-account-draining pain in the ass that has to live in an icebox all summer? Not that I can't be a pain in the ass. I only say that because the inside temperature seems to be one of the things most couples I know argue about."

One more stop in the bedroom to grab my gym bag from my closet, place it next to my work bag (still on the floor next to my sofa) and then I walk into the kitchen. From there I pick up the cats water dish up off the floor (they also have one on the counter...yep, I'm one of those pet owners) and I scrub out that bowl every morning and fill it with fresh water from you guessed it, my Brita pitcher in the refrigerator. Then I double check their dry food and make sure they have enough in their bowls.

(Internal Dialogue) "Where do I begin? My cats are crazy, and I've done nothing but enable them to behave badly. The cats have their side of the counter (and the top of the refrigerator and the top of my kitchen cabinets), and I have my small little square of the counter next to the stove that they're not allowed to walk on and they know it. Either he thinks I'm gross and never marries me or he loves animals just as much as I do, and we find a way to compromise. But right now I'm single, and it is what it is. If I were cooking big elaborate meals, it would be a different story, but I'm not. I don't enjoy cooking big meals for a party of one. So that explains the unused cookbooks and spice rack I mentioned earlier."

I grab a protein bar or shake from the refrigerator and put it in my work bag that I neatly place over my shoulder. The last thing I do is open the living room window blinds behind my sofa because again, my cats are spoiled and they like sunbathing in the window during the day. I shut off the lights in the kitchen, pick up my gym bag, and I'm off to work.

The only thoughts running through my head at this point are anxiety-ridden thoughts about leaving another human being alone with my cats. I love my pets and the thought of them accidentally getting out of my home terrifies me.

In my last relationship, I always stressed to him the importance of doing a head count before leaving the house. It's easy to lock a cat in the closet or bathroom accidentally. I know I'm not the only one that has happened to before, but I've never let one get outdoors. My ex-boyfriend, on the other hand…

One night, we had friends over to my apartment for dinner. The cats were locked in my bedroom just for my own peace of mind. There was one sliding glass door from the bedroom and one in the dining room that both went out to the patio so the cats could remain safely in my bedroom, and we could still access the patio.

I glanced out to the patio and saw my boyfriend tending to the grill. I thought to myself; I don't remember him going out of the dining room door. I walked into the bathroom, which also connected to the bedroom, and noticed the connecting door to the bedroom was open. I felt like a detective at that moment; "He's been through here." I slowly walked into my bedroom and saw the bedroom sliding glass door to the patio was wide open, boyfriend standing by the grill and my cat...low crawling onto the patio. He didn't even notice she was out.

I slowly and calmly walked out onto the patio, so I didn't startle the cat, picked her up, and gave said boyfriend a dirty look. With a stunned look on his face, he quietly said, "Sorry," and I put my cat inside where she belonged, closed the door behind me and locked it. We didn't break up over that, but I was furious. (I read this part of my book to him, and his response was, "You're so dramatic." HA!) But that is a genuine fear I have; which is why "must love animals" is a deal breaker of mine. Don't worry; I'll dish on my deal breakers before this book is finished.

4:30 pm

I walk past my living room window and wave at whichever kitty happens to be sitting in it. As soon as they see me, they jump out of the window. I open the door, and both of them are right there at my feet. I set my work and gym bags on the floor by the sofa and squat down to pet the cats that are meowing and circling my feet. I enthusiastically say, "Look at all these kitties!"

(Internal Dialogue) "Is he going to think I'm completely insane for the way I talk to these cats? I don't care if he does, I'm just wondering."

After petting them for a few seconds, I follow them into the kitchen and pick their bowls up off the floor. I wet a paper towel and wipe up the food mess they made on the floor because I hate a dirty floor. "The kids" then split a can of wet food which keeps them occupied while I run through my after work chores.

First, I put a frying pan on the stove to warm up. By the time I'm done running around my house, I should be ready to fry up a couple of eggs. If I have groceries, I put those away and then make a slow walk through the living room, hallway, and bedroom looking for cat barf. Anybody with cats knows that cat barf is just one of the perks of having cats. I'm pretty lucky in that it's usually only once every couple of weeks.

Once I've cleared the floors of cat barf, I walk into the bathroom and grab the trash can. I empty the bathroom trash into my larger kitchen trash can and then use the smaller one to clean out the litter box.

When I come back inside from walking that out to the dumpster, I take my afternoon vitamins (sitting on the counter next to my morning vitamins) and put the smaller trash can back in the bathroom. I pick my hairdryer off the toilet seat where I left it that morning and put it under the sink. I also straighten up any mess I might have left on the bathroom counter that morning. Then I pick up my clothes off the hallway floor and put them in the hamper. (I don't have a hamper. My hamper is my washing machine. When it's full, I turn it on. And that's how I do laundry.)

(Internal Dialogue) "At some point, he's going to realize that I don't do laundry like an adult; I do laundry like a college student. I have a good reason for it; if I separated my laundry, I would have four small loads to do every week. This way, I have two loads a week. I don't iron any of my clothes either. I've never even owned an iron. I've got to be breaking some sort of unspoken domestic law.

Do I have to turn in my woman card for having never owned an iron?"

The last thing I do is reset my work and gym bags for the morning. I empty my gym bag and put it back in my closet. I then go through my work bag, taking out whatever I need to and put it back on the floor at the end of my sofa.

By now, the pan I put on the stove is hot enough to start my eggs. I add some deli chicken, rice, and cheese to my eggs and take that plate over to the sofa. At this point, I finally shut off my podcasts and turn on Hulu to see what new episodes have popped up in my list.

(Internal Dialogue) "That's right, it's barely 5 pm, and I'm eating dinner. Am I a 70-year-old woman in a retirement community? This is just where I'm at right now. I don't like eating dinner late at night, and I'm usually asleep between 8 and 9 pm so the timing, as of now, makes sense."

I'll usually watch Hulu or Netflix until 7 pm or so. I love television and movies, so there's always something I'm watching whether it's classic television or some new series that has come out on streaming.

When I've had my fill of television, I turn off the TV and any other lights that might be on except for the one over the kitchen sink that stays on overnight. I double check the locks on my doors, close the living room blinds and go into the bedroom and read for an hour, sometimes two; until I'm tired and fall asleep (no later than 9 pm).

I've always been a one book a year reader. In 2018 I made it a goal to read more and read 15 books that year. I usually have one book (fiction or non-fiction) that I'm reading, one self-help book or devotional by Joyce Meyer or some other spiritual leader and whatever book of the Bible I'm currently studying. I've gone from one book a year to several books at a time.

Pretty uneventful at a glance but also uninterrupted. What I do is all completely up to me. I'm reminded of this every time I have a house guest.

My Dallas friend came to town just a few weeks ago. I was in the living room, watching a cooking competition. He was in the bathroom, door open, and his music blaring loud. I started talking to my television because I always talk to my television and I'm not used to anybody being in my space.

Me talking to the show Chopped on television, "Gross, nobody wants to eat that!"

"What?"

"I'm not talking to you."

"What?"

"I'm not talking to you!!"

(He walks into the living room) "What were you saying?"

"I was talking to the television."

"Why?"

(sigh)...so this is what it would be like.

All joking aside; all insecurities, all pet peeves, all *underwear on the floor* and unanswered questions about who this mystery man is. The real question shouldn't be: What part of my routine will annoy this imaginary husband of mine? The real question should be: What do I want my husband to say about me? It's harder than you might think. I had to dig deep, and even still, I'm wondering if I dug deep enough.

"She is a strong woman who is quick to forgive and quick to apologize. She is easy to be with. She loves Jesus, is unshaken in her faith, and takes her relationship with God very seriously. She has a very wide circle of friendships and is accepting of people. She is both fiery and sensitive (sensitive; it's not a bad word. Look up the definition). She is unwavering in her loyalty. You can depend on her. She is smart and funny with a sprinkle of crazy. She loves her family and her friends. She is not afraid to take time for herself and knows how to say no. She is passionate about life. She is not easily offended and painfully self-aware."

What do you want your husband or wife to say about you? Are you that person? We should always be growing and always be teachable, and the good news is, if you aren't the best version of all the things you would like your spouse to say about you one day, you can start changing that now.

There is no perfect person. We are all flawed, and we all have quirks. Some are louder than others, but we do all have them. However, there is a big difference between quirks and character. It's what is in your heart that truly says the most about you.

"...for it is out of the abundance of the heart that the mouth speaks." ~ Jesus Christ, Luke 6:45

CHAPTER TEN

Look at us! We're happy! We have boyfriends!
This is infinitely better than any mood stabilizer I've ever
been on.

~ Paris Geller, Gilmore Girls, the TV show

My friend Pastor Jim once said to me; "You know you have to marry a man that's funny, right? "I know." "The question is, can he be funnier than you?"

Laugher is so important to me. There's something about a man laughing that makes my heart happy. And if I have created that laughter, that's gold! To me, there's a difference between making my girlfriends laugh and making my guy friends laugh. There's a validation that I get when I make a man laugh that I can't quite explain. I could never marry a man who didn't laugh.

My friend Dana, the one I wrote about in chapter two, was one of the funniest people I've ever known. The majority of our time spent together was laughing. It was usually Dana making me laugh. I was almost always the audience when he was in the room, and I gladly took a back seat to his humor. But the times where I genuinely made him laugh gave the quiet comedian trapped inside of me some validation. I loved it when I made him laugh. I miss his laugh.

The man I marry doesn't have to be funny, but he does have to have a sense of humor if he wants to run with my gaggle of semi-certifiably crazy family and friends and me. I want to laugh, and I want to have fun. That might sound unrealistic and not something a typical 40-year-old woman would say, but it's true. If that's not realistic, I'll gladly stay single the rest of my life. That doesn't mean that I don't believe it won't be challenging at times, but I want more fun than challenging.

Can I brag about my brothers-in-law for a minute? Matt and JP are two of the most laid back, down for anything guys I've ever met. One summer, I was in town for my annual trip to the Minnesota State Fair. My youngest sister Melinda, who is the craziest of us three, decided we all needed matching outfits for the fair.

We went to Walmart, and Melinda found these horrible t-shirts that had several pictures of cat faces all over the front. Not cartoon cats, actual photographs of cat faces. We took them home, and I watched my sisters present them to their husbands.

Their response: "Yes! We are going to look so rad at the fair!" We had so much fun that day at the fair in our horrible, trashy cat t-shirts.

I can't be with somebody who won't roll with something like that. Did any of us think these were cool shirts? Of course not; they were awful. We got them because we thought it would be funny and if we could get some reactions from strangers, then that was the icing on the cake for us. We are a family that will do anything for a laugh.

That same year at the Fair, my sister Melinda got one of those weird wooden back scratchers. It looks like a yardstick with little fingers on the end. She walked up behind a couple of teenagers (that she did not know) and started scratching their backs with it. When they turned around, my sister said with a straight face, "Don't make it weird."

These are the kind of shenanigans my family voluntarily gets themselves into. We have a lot of fun together. You can't be uptight and be a part of my family. I don't see how that could ever work.

Before I met my wife, I was 90% happy. Now I know a relationship can make me 100% happy, but it can also make me 100% unhappy.

~ Josh Wolf, from the podcast, Prinze and The Wolf

So, why not try online dating? It's simple; I don't want to. I am fully aware and often reminded, that if I were to create an online profile, the odds of me finding somebody would significantly increase.

I had one friend who online dated for six months. One night over dinner she sobbed about how exhausting it was going out with guy after guy and nothing was working out. I finally asked her, "Why are you doing this to yourself? You know you don't have to keep doing this." She was already upset, and my question didn't make it any better. She got very defensive and said that she can't stop if she ever wants to meet somebody.

It appeared to be her life goal to find a husband, but she was sacrificing so much peace in that search. She wasn't happy. I'm not doing that to myself. I'm not saying that everybody who online dates is that manic, but if you're not having fun online dating then stop it. It's supposed to be a fun, casual adventure with the possibility of finding somebody you connect with. Not a life-sucking nightmare.

I can't speak for men, but as women, we are already so hard on ourselves. I've never liked my front teeth. They were short, discolored and riddled with fillings. Coming from somebody who loves to laugh and smile, that's a problem.

In 2018 I did something about it. After several dentist appointments and four thousand dollars later, I now have a perfect smile courtesy of five new crowns.

The things I've heard some people say about the men and women they find online are so mean. "His teeth are so gross." "He was so ugly." "He looks like a pedophile." I'm not making those up. I heard them all, and it was disturbing.

Why would I want to expose myself to this type of criticism? I'm hard enough on myself. I don't need some stranger to point out every imperfection I have. In the very next breath, after shredding several people they don't know and have never met in person, now they turn on themselves. "I messaged a couple of guys online, and they never wrote me back. It's probably because I'm not pretty enough. They're way too cute to be interested in me."

I know it's not like that for everybody. I have a small, and I mean very small number of friends who were successful at online dating, but I have far more who have had disappointing date after disappointing date, and it's made them judgmental; about the men who are asking them out and about how they see themselves.

It's hard for me to sit through these conversations having my own insecurities. "His teeth are so gross." And then people wonder why I spent thousands of dollars fixing my teeth. Don't misunderstand me; the number one reason I fixed them was for me, but listening to people point out physical imperfections in other people only made me think more about my own.

(Internal Dialogue): "You see? People did notice your teeth. Thank god you got those fixed. Too bad you can't fix your hair...and you'll never be happy with your body so nobody else will either."

Strong (definition): Having the ability to bear or endure, able to sustain attacks, having virtues of great efficacy, full of spirit, intoxicating, not easily overthrown or altered, having great force of mind, comprising much in few words, bright, glaring vivid

One day over lunch, a friend of mine told me I had a strong personality. It wasn't so much what she said, but the wide-eyed, slow nod of her head reaction when I responded with, "I do?" She said it wasn't a bad thing. (Could have fooled me) It just meant I have strong convictions. So now I'm on a mission to dissect what all of this means.

I went to my friend Pastor Jim later that night and asked him if he thought I had a strong personality. With no hesitation, he said, "You absolutely do." (Oh great) I told him it sounds like a bad thing. He said, "No, it just means that you have strong convictions and the man that dates you will have to be a real man. There's nothing wrong with that."

If both these friends are saying I have a strong personality, and there's nothing wrong with that, then clearly, there is something wrong with my definition of the word "strong." When I hear "you have a strong personality," my internal dialogue says, you're difficult to be with, you're not a good listener, and you're hard to talk to, and I don't think I'm any of that.

While obsessing over why "strong personality" bothered me so much and because clearly, I couldn't let it go, I talked to yet another friend, she said when in doubt look up the definition of the word. Later that week, she told me there were 22 definitions of the word strong, and she thinks 14 of them apply to me.

And guess what? None of those definitions sounded pushy or negative. Actually, those definitions made me glad I have a strong personality. They made me feel proud of the woman I have become over the years.

When in doubt, look up the definition.

In chapter 6, I talked about my greatest fear about being the last one single. Believe it or not, I also have a fear of getting married. I'm terrified of being left. I didn't end my two long-term relationships, they did. Some of my most heartbreaking friendships that ended were not ended by me.

(Internal Dialogue) "That's your thing. You're the one who people leave. In your wildest imagination, can you ever imagine *any* man wanting to spend the rest of their life with you? Yeah, me either."

That's rough right? But it's what goes through my head. Even though I don't believe this in my heart to be true, it's sometimes what I say, and it's sometimes how I feel. Getting hurt can leave some pretty gnarly scars. Giving your heart to somebody is really scary, which is why I take it so seriously.

I'm not looking for a project. You have to have your life together, and you have to have a dream.

~ my strong, awesome, single friend Ashlee

So what do I want? It's a loaded question. I know people that have "the list." I have nothing against having a list unless it's loaded with superficial things like hair color and what type of job he has. Some people have a very specific type they're attracted to. I am all over the board. I can find a man with tattoos, a motorcycle and works on cars for a living just as attractive as a man who wears a suit and works in an office. Sure physical appearance plays a part initially, but its character that truly attracts me and should be what attracts all of us....or turns us off.

One Sunday morning, Pastor Jim was talking about praying with a closed fist vs. an open hand. He said, and I'm paraphrasing, "We are always telling God what we want, but only God knows what we need. It's okay to tell God what you want as long as you're praying with an open hand, but most of us pray with a closed fist. If we don't learn to say, God, *Your will* be done; eventually, God will say, fine, *your will* be done."

I used to have a list. I threw it out after listening to that sermon. I'm not by any means suggesting that you all toss your list of what you are looking for, but for me, I had already failed twice doing it my way. Clearly, I didn't know what I was doing. Tossing that list was my way of telling God that I wanted who HE had for me. Not who I thought I wanted.

My list now is very small and all in my head. It's also evolved over time. As I've grown through this process, I have learned more about what my heart requires. I'm not going to bore you with every deal breaker I have, but I'll share a few with you. I hope this encourages you to look deeper into what it is you are looking for in your own life.

1. God must come first. Period. I will be friends with anybody, but I won't marry anybody. I'm also not interested in changing somebody, so he has to already be grounded and unshaken in his faith.
   Jesus replied, "You must love the Lord your God with all your heart, all your soul, and all your mind. This is the first and greatest commandment. A second is equally important: Love your neighbor as yourself." ~ Matthew 22:36-40
   This verse leads me right into my second deal breaker.

2. I have no time for rude or disrespectful; how he treats other people and me. Being short with a waitress at a restaurant, being completely unaware of the people around him and being disrespectful of different cultures or orientations. Like I said before, I will be friends with anybody, so my circle of friends is wide. I am a Christian, a devoted follower of Jesus but not everybody I am friends with shares that belief. I have friends from all walks of life; all religions, all orientations. If you're a good person, I'll be friends with you. If you're not comfortable having a circle of friends that is that broad, that's okay. And as long as you are not a hateful person,

145

I'll be friends with you too, but I won't marry you. My friends are very important to me. If he doesn't want to get to know and spend time with the people that I love, then he isn't the one for me. If he is completely unaware of the people around him and rude, I'm cutting him loose. Can't do it; won't do it.

3. Must love animals! I can promise you there will always be a revolving door of cats and dogs in my house, and he has to be okay with that. Of course, I would prefer that he is totally on board with it, but that isn't a deal breaker. That doesn't mean I don't love kids. Between my two sisters, I have two nieces and three nephews who LOVE their crazy auntie Stephie and I am crazy about them! But there is no biological clock that is driving me to find "the one" and get married as fast as possible.

Somebody once told me, "Never say never. That's usually when God makes you do that thing you said you would never do." Look, I am completely open to the fact that I could meet somebody tomorrow and totally change my mind and suddenly develop a desire to have kids. I am fully aware that is a possibility. But right now, what would be fulfilling for me (instead of getting pregnant in my 40's) is to get involved in some sort of mentoring program with foster kids who have no functional mother or father in their lives.

Being in an environment where I could pour into the lives of several foster kids or even aged out foster kids who need somebody to believe in them or encourage them or point them in the right direction truly makes my heart happy. There are so many kids out there with no parents or family at all who need people to invest in their lives. What an amazing opportunity that would be!

There's also the possibility the guy I marry might already have kids. If he has kids, that is not a deal breaker. What kind of a person would I be if I couldn't love the children of the man I chose to be with? How could I not love something that is a part of him? I've talked to some amazing friends who have opened my eyes to the importance of being a step-mom if that's something God has for me. It's painful for me to think that there are kids out there who have step-parents who see them only as an inconvenience. If the man I marry has kids, I would never want to make them feel that way.

But I will always have a lot of love for animals. I would love to one day to rescue senior dogs in shelters. I also love cats because cats are easy and have big personalities. Where a dog is loyal no matter what, I fully believe if a cat were able to flip you the middle finger, it totally would and that cracks me up!

Adorable old church man: "Young lady, are you married?"

Me: "No, I'm not."

Adorable old church man: "A beautiful young woman like you not married? Well, don't you worry, you'll find him."

Me: "I'm busy; he will have to find me."

I want a man who knows what he wants. But Stephanie, what if he's shy? Then he will find a way to get over it, or he will move on to somebody else. It's that simple. I have no problem giving a man a clue that I'm interested in him. Not that I'm an expert in that area which I have proven not to be in previous chapters, but I don't want to make the first move. And by the first move, I mean the one that takes the current state of the relationship to the next level. He will have to level up. After that, it's game on for me! But that initial level up move needs to come from him.

Just so we are clear, I am fully aware I am a bit old school in a world that doesn't typically work that way anymore. Most people meet online nowadays. That's cool. I know a lot of women who level up their relationships before the guys do. Fine, you do you. But that's not me. Not this time around. I don't want to be the one to level up. My heart wants him to come after me. If I make the first move, my heart will always wonder if I had just waited a little bit longer, would he have made a move.

Listen, I spent more than half my life manufacturing relationships out of a deeply rooted fear of being alone. There was no time to pray about it or ask God what He thought. Which means I also didn't trust God. I had to make it happen myself. I wasted so much time trying to be who I thought they all wanted me to be so that I could say I had somebody. There was absolutely nothing organic about what I was doing. I worked so hard silently convincing them that I was worth it and all the while believing myself that I wasn't. That's just so gross.

It's because of those bad decisions from years past that I feel it's time for me to wait. If I make the first move on somebody I'm interested in I'm going to feel like the old me who was too impatient to let it play itself out. And I'm not that woman anymore. This woman loves herself and knows her value.

I'm also not waiting for "the one" because I don't think there is just one person out there for me or anybody for that matter. I believe there are many men in this world that I could connect with and have an amazing life and marriage with. There have been several men in the last few years that I would have loved for them to level me up. That's right, several! It wasn't a question of which one do I

148

want, but more a question of...which one is going to bite first?

I am not in the business of lining up a bunch of men and trying to find out which one out of the group I like the best. I'll never make a man compete for my attention with another man. It needs to be authentic. Even if I have a few men in mind and I might like them all for very different reasons, the *only* thing I am waiting for is to see which one will level me up first. From there, assuming I am also interested, I am all in on getting to know that one better and the rest will be officially off the table.

Yes, this world is changing, and the way people meet is changing as well, but I fully believe with all my heart that if a man hears from God, he will waste no time when God says, "You like her? You have my blessing. Go get her!" Either you want to get to know me, or you don't. It is that simple. And while the world is always changing, do you know who never changes? God. And I believe my heart is right in this decision to wait.

God is bigger than my insecurities and thank God He is bigger than my moments of being completely oblivious to a man who might be interested in me. I honestly believe because my heart is right, if I happen to miss a moment where a man was trying to level up, God will be right there to bring it back around again. Thank God He knows my heart. The Bible says, *"No good thing does he withhold from those who walk uprightly."* To me, in this scenario, that means if I miss a move, God's got me!

I spent the last ten years of my life discovering what I wanted, what I needed, and more importantly, who I wanted to be; as a woman of God and as a wife. I've been told many times that I need to "put myself out there more." I don't even know what that means. I am as "out there," as I'm going to be. Between church, the gym, dinners out with friends, the Improv and many other super fun things I do to enjoy my life, I am as "out there" as I'm going to be. I will never intentionally insert myself into something for the sole purpose of meeting somebody. I think that's weird and again, reminds me of the old me.

You don't have to do it that way, but that's the way I'm doing it. I have never had that exchange before with somebody I was interested in, and I want that badly. I have many friends who think this whole thing is bonkers but guess what? This Stephanie doesn't give a rip what people think. Again, I'm not telling you this is the ONLY way; this is MY way. Is it easy to wait? Hell no! It's really hard sometimes. But I believe it'll be worth it. I also think that when it does happen and it will, it'll make a really great book. =)

With that said, he has to meet my standards. I won't fall all over any man simply because he pursues me. If he doesn't meet my standards, then it's been real. You shouldn't treat dating like a marriage. If somebody is exhibiting horrible behavior (and I'm talking to men and women here) and many attempts to address it aren't changing it, it's time go. We are talking about the rest of my life...forever changing the rest of my life! He has to be extraordinary! I hope that doesn't sound too intense, but I have watched too many men and women make compromises they shouldn't be making where their relationships are concerned.

I'm watching for his character. Is he kind? Does he have empathy? When things get rough, does he press into God and the people he loves, or does he withdraw? DOES HE LIKE TO LAUGH? How does he treat me in front of *his* friends? How does he treat me in front of *my* friends? I also want to know what my inner circle of friends and family thinks about him? How does he feel about them?

These are all things that might take some time to find out, but I'm talking about attaching my life to this person. That is nothing to take lightly.

I want somebody who doesn't make me miss being single. If my life isn't better with him, then I'm settling. And I don't want to settle. If I can't have a man who loves me intensely, is fiercely protective and loyal without wavering, then I don't want it at all. I love my life. I'll only invite somebody into it if he makes my life better.

I know what you're wondering. Why is it okay for me to expect so much from the person I marry? The answer is simple; because I also bring all of that to the table. I demand loyalty because I am loyal. I demand respect because I am respectful. I don't expect anything out of a friendship or relationship that I can't also provide for that person. I should be the safest person on planet earth for my husband to talk to without fear of rejection or judgment. And I want him to be that for me. That does not mean I'm perfect or that I expect him to be, but I do pride myself on being stable, and stability in any relationship is very important.

When you look back on your life, the only thing that matters is did you spend it doing what you love with the people you love. Were you happy? Did you make the most of this beautiful, terrifying, and messed up life? Did you let go of all the things that held you back so you can hold on to what matters most?

~ Miranda Bailey, Grey's Anatomy

It was quite a process getting from where I was to where I am now. Where am I? I am a happy, content, single woman who is waiting for no one to enjoy my life! What's next for me? I would love to get back to directing. I remember the morning I walked into my new church (which is significantly smaller than my old church), and I saw they had installed cameras. My eyes got real wide, and my heart skipped a beat, and immediately, the Holy Spirit said to me, "Is your book done?" "No." "Then sit down." I did, however, introduce myself to the media team, and I have an open invitation to shadow them whenever I'm ready. I assure you, dear reader, that my love for media is still there and I will return to it.

This has given me the freedom to fully enjoy my life. I don't want to live my life wishing I was in the next phase. I refuse to be so focused on what *could be* that I completely miss where I'm at. I don't want to be that person who looks back on her single years and only see the sadness and many nights crying myself to sleep. Life is too short for that.

When that relationship does find me, I want to look back on my singles years and smile. I want to look back on those years that most people waste away and say, I had fun! I traveled! I saw my favorite bands in concert! I went to the Improv and met my favorite comics. I went to Oregon and ran barefoot on the beach. I went to Las Vegas and spent some money on myself.

I want to have fun being fully present and enjoying this phase of my life because when that relationship does come, everything will change. I'll have fun there too, but I want it to be a brand new adventure. Not a feeling of FINALLY, I'm not single anymore. It's simply, the next phase. And I get to enjoy that phase with somebody new.

How do you know when you find real love? Here is part of the answer to that question: When you find someone who will sacrifice for you more than anyone else will. Real love requires real sacrifice.

~ Pastor Preston Morrison, Gateway Church, Scottsdale

Stephanie has worked steadily in the insurance industry since 1998. This not only pays the bills but has allowed her to pursue her creative side. In addition to her full time job and writing her first book, Stephanie is also a Video Director and camera operator at her church. She loves to read, travel and is passionate about rescue animals, television, movies, and sarcasm.

Born and raised in Minnesota, Stephanie has lived in Phoenix, Arizona since 2002 with a revolving door of adopted pets. She is fully embracing this season of her life, and hopes to inspire others to do the same. She currently lives with her two tan tabby cats, Simone & Sipowicz...not to be confused with the two cats in the above picture. Those belong to her sister, Melinda. (Fiona & Toby)

Thank you for reading!

If you enjoyed this book and would like to leave a review on Amazon, that would be awesome =)

Find me on Instagram @stef_mills or email me at info@stephaniemillsbooks.com

53243427R00095

Made in the USA
Lexington, KY
27 September 2019